TWENTY-SEVEN YEARS IN ALASKA

TRUE STORIES OF ADVENTURE IN THE ALASKAN WILDERNESS

by Jennifer Hellings

This Belongs To:

Beatrice

Twenty Seven Years in Alaska
Copyright 2015 by Jennifer Hellings

Tellwell Talent
www.tellwell.ca

ISBN
Paperback: 978-1-987985-32-0
Hardcover: 978-1-987985-31-3
eBook: 978-1-987985-30-6

CONTENTS

TWENTY-SEVEN
YEARS IN
ALASKA

CHAPTER ONE

THE ODDS ARE GOOD, BUT THE GOODS ARE ODD.

ALASKAN LICENSE PLATES DECLARE THAT ALASKA IS "THE Last Frontier" and many hardy souls are attracted to the state for this very reason. They come from all over the United States and from many other countries to try their hand at living closer to the land. They are looking for a wild place where there are fewer restrictions, fewer rules, and fewer society mores with which to contend. It is true that in many places in rural Alaska - certainly in the wilderness - there are few to no building codes, no permits to acquire, and no regulations to follow. People can buy land very cheaply and then do with it what they will. These adventuresome souls are free to build any kind of ramshackle dwelling on their property as they try to eke out a living off the land. But

Nature is her own enforcer in the North, and many newcomers give up after their first winter. Spring is called "break-up". While this technically refers to the departure of ice and snow, it also seems to denote the many relationships which shatter with the spring melt as people rush to escape the confines of a relationship which drove them crazy during the long winter months. The ones who stay have a tendency to be tough, independent, innovative, and willing to do without the niceties of civilization.

In towns such as Homer on Kachemak Bay which has a winter population of about 4,000, there is often a gender divide with a 4:1 ratio of men to women. This has led to a few coarse but accurate sayings. A woman's dating chances in Homer are described as follows: "The odds are good, but the goods are odd." A woman might find that she has many opportunities in the form of single men, but she might find she does not want to keep any of the treasures she finds.

A friend of mine described one such date, which I consider instructive for any woman thinking of heading to the last frontier to catch a man. Susan had a professional job in town which allowed her to go to work wearing shoes instead of gum boots, and she even wore the occasional skirt. She was an attractive woman, and being single, she was noticed by men. One of these men asked her to go out with him on a dinner date. Thinking he would take her to one of the restaurants in town, she put on a skirt and even some high heeled shoes, which he noticed appreciatively when he picked her up. Most women do not wear heels in small towns, because there is a limited amount of sidewalk and pavement with most of the roads and parking lots being made of gravel or dirt. Heeled shoes are made for the city. They sink into gravel, to say nothing of dirt or mud. Still, my friend had put her best foot forward, so to speak, and she assumed her date would offer her his arm if need be. Unfortunately, she was about to experience a "date" with one of the men who had fled civilization because he had never quite fit in. He had never learned to navigate the etiquette of taking a woman in a skirt out to dinner.

He arrived in his pickup truck; so far so good. Pickup trucks are the standard vehicle in rural Alaska. Unfortunately, things started to go downhill from there. He took her to a roadside burger joint which lacked any tables and chairs. This establishment was more like a drive-up window on the road leading to the harbor where people heading out to work on their boats could catch a bite to eat. But the food was good, and she was a flexible Alaskan lady, so she made no complaints about eating a burger on her lap while sitting in the cab of her date's truck. He then decided they would "go for a drive", and proceeded to take her over rough gravel roads which wound through the hills and the area surrounding the town. While driving he talked non-stop of his commercial fishing career. After some time, Susan began to feel the need to use a washroom. Gentle hints given to her date were left unnoticed, as he was too focused on discussing fishing. Eventually she had to cry: "Stop the car!" after which she hopped out and scrambled off into the woods to relieve herself behind the nearest bush, her high heels digging little post holes in the dirt as she went. By the time she returned to his truck her nylons were in tatters; however, her date seemed not to notice, as he continued his soliloquy on fishing.

Finally the interminable evening came to an end. Her date was talked out, and he returned the way he had come to take her home. This is where things began to get awkward. As she attempted to make her civil goodbyes, he showed some surprise that she was not inviting him in. He had had a wonderful time; what was the problem? She politely tried to give him the speech on how they could be friends, but they did not have that much in common, etc., etc. He began to protest. Hadn't he bought her a lovely dinner? Hadn't he explained what a successful fisherman he was? When she remained firm in her farewell, he decided to pull out all the stops in his efforts to charm her: "But I've got halibut!" he cried. In essence, he promised to supply her with some, should they become lovers. Too stunned and amazed to even be offended, Susan escaped that pickup truck. Yes, indeed, she had met a real Alaskan man, who seemed to think that offering an exchange of halibut for sex was a good deal she could not refuse.

The types of living accommodations where people wait out the winter are truly astonishing. A friend of mine named John spent a couple of years living in an old school bus parked on the road at the edge of a property on the outskirts of town. When the weather grew cold I became concerned about him, but he said that the wood stove in that bus would run him right out of it once he got it going. I knew of another young man named Daniel who lived in a small camper, the kind that is designed to sit on the back of a medium-sized pickup truck - only he was minus the truck. His camper was parked on a windswept spit of land sticking out into the ocean. When the snow arrived his only means of escape was to trudge through the deep snow to the edge of the nearest road and walk or hitchhike to town.

One particularly notorious character lived up in the hills in a log cabin. He could be seen regularly coming down the mountain on his way to town with his black dog trotting by his side. No one knew too much about him since he stuck to himself, but he eventually became rather famous when he was featured in a newspaper article. He had drawn attention to himself by firing shots at his nearest neighbors. They had apparently annoyed him by traveling too close to his property on their snow machine. He objected to the machine because it was too noisy, and his reaction was to fire shots at the neighbors in protest. When the Alaska State Troopers became involved, it was discovered that he was living in a cabin with upwards of seventy chickens with which he shared living space and warmth. No one was sure if he regarded the chickens as a food source or perhaps just as friends.

Yes, sir, housing can be found for a very low price in rural Alaska, and the authorities will pretty much let you do what you want if you keep a low profile. If you are tough, and you do not mind living without running water, central heating, or having something besides dirt as your floor, then you can survive in the bush with a very limited cash flow. While it is true that there are a lot of single men up in the North Country, a woman would be well-advised to do a little soul searching as to her own priorities before she travels to Alaska to catch a man.

CHAPTER TWO

HOW I CAME TO ALASKA

PEOPLE COME TO ALASKA FOR ALL SORTS OF REASONS, AND I guess mine are no more or less strange than any others. My father was an international airline pilot who flew all over the world for a couple of different airlines. His last job as a pilot was flying DC-8 planes as a captain for Japan Airlines. After many years of living overseas in Tokyo, Japan Airlines transferred my father to Anchorage, Alaska. Consequently our family moved with him. Anchorage is a busy international airport used for the refueling of planes on route to locations all over the world. There was a certain poetry and symmetry in our family moving to Anchorage for my father's last posting. My mother had been a stewardess when my parents met. At that time both of my parents were flying for Canadian Pacific Airlines, since they were both Canadian. The symmetry came from the fact that my parents met on Shemya Island, a godforsaken rock in the middle of the ocean at the end of the long archipelago which forms the Aleutian chain of islands off Alaska's coast. The weather is terrible out on Shemya, and crews would often find themselves stranded by weather conditions for days at a time. They had nothing to do but drink and socialize in the rudimentary barracks while they waited for the weather to clear. Being stranded out there together for several days, my parents became friends. Even more ironic is the fact that my mother told me that when she was flying in and out of Anchorage in the early 50s she would look out of the window of the plane at the frozen town below, thinking it was a barren, forbidding place, and somewhere she would never want to live. Yet they returned, and both of my parents lived the remainder of their lives in Anchorage. I was sixteen when my family moved to Anchorage in 1975, and I stayed in Alaska for twenty-seven years.

CHAPTER THREE

BUILDING A CABIN IN THE WOODS

I MET DAVID IN 1990 WHEN WE WERE BOTH LIVING IN Anchorage. He was working as a welder at a local welding shop, and I was finishing my graduate degree at university in preparation for a planned move back to my native Canada. Meeting David changed those plans, and I stayed in Alaska for another twelve years. Since neither of us were city folk, we discussed where we might like to live. We eventually agreed on a place called Homer, at the end of the Kenai Peninsula, two hundred and twenty miles south of Anchorage. We soon secured employment and were able to go ahead with our move. Both of us, however, wanted to get "further off the grid", a phrase used to describe people who crave a life in the wilderness. We wanted to get away from the constant buzz of civilization. I find that the further I am from civilization, the more my body and my mind seem to slow down as I synchronize with the ebb and flow of tide and current, wind and wave. Something inside of me settles into a peace, which I cannot find rushing around in my normal life. I imagine everyone who is drawn to the wilderness will know just what I mean. Perhaps we all go out there for the same reason: to connect with something deep inside ourselves, deep inside the earth. Conversation dwindles, and long moments of time are spent together in comfortable silence, breathing with the rhythm of nature. For this reason, I do not understand those who bring radios, music, or other forms of electronics into the wild. It seems to me they are missing more than half of the experience. I choose to share the outdoors with people who enjoy it the same way I do, because it feeds something deep in our souls.

In the spring of 1996 we were finally able to purchase our own piece of land on the far side of Kachemak Bay, the body of water upon which Homer sits. Kachemak Bay is a stunningly beautiful place. We owned two-and-a-half acres of pristine wilderness in a place called Bear Cove located a fourteen-mile boat ride from the nearest harbor in the small town of Homer. We had a twenty-six foot boat - an aluminum skiff complete with a small turtle-back cabin. The Guinevere was a mostly flat-bottomed skiff sporting only a small V in the hull at the bow. The aft portion of the hull was almost completely flat. Our commode was a bucket with a fancy snap-on plastic seat shaped like a regular toilet seat for comfort. With these rudiments of civilization, we set out to build our dream cabin in the Alaskan woods. Our building site was covered in tall trees and almost impassable undergrowth. The forest floor was littered with fallen trees which had blown down when they grew too tall to support their weight in the thin coastal soil. The area had also been ravaged by the spruce bark beetle, insects which eat the living layer in the bark, thereby killing the tree but leaving it standing. Unfortunately, this standing dead wood is almost useless for lumber and poses a real threat to humans and animals alike. The giant trees can fall or break off halfway up from only a moderate wind. Sometimes these fifty-foot sections of trees would become hung-up in the branches of other trees, suspended, until a slight wind from the opposite direction brought them crashing down. These broken trees are called "widow makers" for their tragic consequences.

Even so, it was our dream to build a cabin on this remote site. A stream of glacial meltwater ran down the mountain to the ocean's edge, a close boat ride away from our property. From this stream we could collect the purest drinking water. We slowly carved out access to our piece of land, starting with the shoreline, by removing logs that had accumulated over the years. This would enable us to reach the shore with our boat, where we could then off-load our gear. Clearing this shoreline took many days which we affectionately referred to as our "boat rodeo". Sometimes we moved a log, only to have it come drifting back on the next high tide. This was a highly unwelcome sight to be sure after all of our hard work, as it frequently took us hours just to move one log. We had to learn the patterns of tides and currents to find a spot where we could tow the logs without having them come drifting back. These logs were a serious navigation hazard to us and everyone else when they were floating free on the current.

View of Kachemak Bay and Bear Cove from opposite side of the bay.

We were in Kachemak Bay, which is part of the Cook Inlet drainage. There is a twenty-six foot tidal differential in this bay between the highest and lowest tides, second in height only to the Bay of Fundy in Canada. After several days of work, we were able to access our shoreline and off-load our equipment. The Guinevere was a rough-riding boat, to be sure, and she would jar one's teeth out of one's sockets if there was only a small chop on the ocean, particularly when the intervals between the waves were short. Still, she suited our purposes perfectly, because we could land her right on the shore. Her sturdy, aluminum hull would not be damaged as she rested in the rocks and barnacles at the water's edge.

We spent every spare moment of several years working up in Bear Cove to build our cabin. The rest of the time I was in Homer, where I had a full-time job. We owned a traditional style house in town which included indoor plumbing and central heating. David worked as a marine welder for a fuel barge company that delivered home heating oil to the many far-flung villages of Alaska. He was out of town a lot in the summer months, and I stayed behind. This is a standard pattern in Homer. Women often work in town, while the men work out of town in various trades: commercial fishing, oil field work, mining, logging, and the many support industries that make life in the North possible. Whenever we could get away from our respective jobs, we would travel by boat up to Bear Cove to work on our land. We slept quite comfortably on our boat, which made our time on the land much more productive.

The Guinevere with kayak alongside.

Logging up in Bear Cove was a hair-raising experience. David took down the trees one by one with an enormous chainsaw. I would stand far enough away to be safe no matter which direction the tree fell, holding tightly to the collars of our two German Shepherds, Tasha and Mariah. I prayed for David's safety. Anyone who has taken down large trees with just a chainsaw knows that despite one's best efforts and calculations, sometimes the fall does not go the way one plans. The method commonly used is to cut a wedge in the tree on the side one wishes the tree to fall, and then to cut the trunk through from the other side. This works perfectly in theory; however, sometimes the top branches of a tree provide a counterweight in the opposite direction. A tree-faller always tries to anticipate this, and often trees are climbed with spike boots and a harness to remove big branches before the main trunk is severed. In this way, the unpredictability of that counterweight can be avoided. David and I did not have this equipment, hence the anxiety and the prayers.

I remember one particularly huge tree that was over one hundred feet tall. This tree was close to our landing spot and it had to go, but it truly was a giant topped with a huge crown of thick branches. David had skinned off the lower branches to make the fall as safe as possible, but it was still a dangerous job. I watched anxiously with the dogs from a nearby slope. First, David cut a deep wedge in the tree. This act is always hazardous, since there is the very real possibility that the tree will give way at this point while the logger is standing right where the tree falls. Still, it is the best method for cutting down a tree by oneself without the aid of big, fancy equipment. After cutting the wedge, David went around to the other side of the tree and began cutting through the massive trunk. He cut the tree all the way through, and still it stood there. We now had a one-hundred-foot tree, standing, but completely sheared off at the base. We were in an incredibly dangerous situation. We both looked on incredulously. Now what? I prayed; the dogs whined; and David just stood there, holding his breath. After a few interminable seconds, a slight breeze came up, and suddenly the mighty tree came crashing down with a boom like thunder. It hit the earth, sending a shudder through the ground. David told me afterwards that when the tree was finally at rest on the earth, he almost threw up, so great was his fear and his relief. Logging in remote parts of Alaska is not for the faint of heart.

The extreme tides in Kachemak Bay present both a great opportunity and a great hazard to those on the ocean. We quickly learned to never do anything on or near the ocean without consulting a tide book first. These are conveniently printed and distributed by many stores in the little town of Homer, the base of our departures. Our little bay was a small pocket off the larger Bear Cove, and we liked to call it "Starlight Bay". There the water would completely disappear on the lowest tides about once per month. Since our boat had an almost flat bottom, we could let her beach herself without incurring any damage. This did mean, however, that we were not going anywhere until the water came back, a fact which had to be remembered in case of injury. Rushing off to the hospital to seek medical attention was not going to be possible a lot of the time. One is truly on one's own in most parts of rural Alaska. We were aware of this fact, and we always tried be careful and to play it safe. The nickname "Starlight Bay" was a reference to the bio-luminescent plankton which frequently accumulated in the water. Stirring the water at night caused the little creatures to light up, and the water would glow and sparkle anywhere it was disturbed. There is so much beauty in the wilderness I was often left speechless with wonder.

One of the advantages of the tide going so far out was being able to work in the mud to set a permanent anchor for our boat in our little bay from which we attached a mooring buoy. We would tie up to our mooring buoy at night. We also added a running line for both safety and convenience. With this device we could pull the boat out to rest at the mooring buoy after off-loading gear on the shore, and thus keep the boat afloat as much as possible. A running line is a triangular pulley system with two points anchored on the shore and one point anchored at the buoy. The rope is a large loop, so by pulling the rope one direction, we could bring the boat towards shore. By pulling the rope the other direction, we could pull the boat back out to sea. This was a great system which provided an extra measure of flexibility regarding our comings and goings from Bear Cove. Since the tide only went out completely once or twice per month, most of the time we had a floating boat.

During one of our trips we knew we would be dealing with an

extreme low tide in which the water would completely leave our mooring area. We were not too concerned, however, since this low tide would be happening in the middle of the night, and so by the time we were ready to get up in the morning, most of the water would have returned. We retired for the night, securely fastened to our buoy and expecting the little cove to become dry by the middle of the night when our flat-bottomed boat would rest comfortably on the mud until morning. Things did not go quite as we planned.

In the middle of the night, David and I both woke up to the sensation of our boat tilting at an odd angle. Something was wrong. David sprang out of bed and rushed to the side of the boat, but it was too late. Our boat was in the process of settling on a large rock, and the angle at which it was tilting was becoming more and more pronounced by the second. Our little bay was an expanse of flat mud with the exception of one large rock, and we had found it. As the tilt grew steeper and steeper, we quickly realized we would have to abandon ship. We gathered our gear, put on our warm clothes, and climbed overboard. The mud was deeper than our boots, but there was no help for it. We slogged to the shoreline. David even had to carry the dogs through the worst of it for fear they would get stuck.

We eventually made it safely to shore. It was summer time, so the short night had already given way to dawn. In the early morning light we gazed at our boat with trepidation. It was sitting at a steep angle now, one side up and one side down. We wondered what would happen when the water came back. Would the boat right herself and float, or would it fill with water instead? We just didn't know, and we had about six hours to wait and find out.

Happily for us, when the water came back our good little boat righted herself. We had escaped without any damage, except to our egos. If our boat had swamped, we would have been stranded. There is no way one could walk out for help from where we were; the terrain is too impassable, and we were too far from any other people. We did have a cellular phone with us: an old fashioned, satchel phone was the technology of the time. But, as is true in so many parts of the wilderness, there was no easy way to get a signal. We had found that if we climbed to the top of the nearest steep hilltop, then stood on a stump, and then held the phone over our heads, sometimes we would get a signal, but not always. We could call the Coast Guard or another boat from our VHF radio on the boat, but this would have been very hard to do if our boat had filled up with water.

Fortunately that did not happen, and we were able to hold on to some of our pride when the Guinevere righted herself. Needless to say, our first project was moving that darn anchor so that next time we would be out of harm's way. This was no small feat, as we had done a very good job of securing it the first time. Eventually the anchor was moved, new lines were secured, and we felt reasonably safe in the belief that we would not have a repeat performance of our boat-tipping adventure. I guess we learned what most mariners learn sooner or later: boats and rocks are like magnets to each other. If there is just one rock in an area, be careful, because your boat will find it.

CHAPTER FOUR

A SPRING HIKE

WE WORKED IN BEAR COVE DURING EVERY SEASON, WITH the exception of December and January when the lack of daylight coupled with the cold temperatures made the trip just too arduous. Throughout the year, however, we would sometimes take breaks from our building project and find other ways to enjoy the wilderness.

When spring finally comes to south central Alaska, it is something to savor, so one year we headed off into the hills above town for a hike. The birch trees had burst into color, leafing out all at once in a glorious spring green. The tender shoots of "Devil's Club" were coming up everywhere, tempting humans and animals alike to fill their bellies after a hungry winter. Being covered in nasty spikes which cause a terrible itching when they meet human flesh, this five-foot prickly plant is the bane of many a wilderness wanderer. However, when it first pokes its head above ground in the spring it is tender and succulent, and moose, bear, and humans can feast. The snow was gone except for the piles left when the roads were plowed, and the moose cows were calving up in the hills. It was a perfect spring day in mid-May. We found a snow machine trail, clear of snow, with the spring melt filling puddles in the tracks. Everything was coming back to life after a long winter sleep. Many small birds had returned to the north, and the trees were full of song. It was warm, with temperatures in the mid-50s during the day, but still cold enough at night that the mosquitoes were not yet plentiful. They had not reached the density they would maintain in the summer months, when hungry swarms can stampede a herd of caribou, desperate to get away from the incessant buzz of the blood sucking creatures.

We parked our car at a wide spot on a gravel road above town, unloaded Tasha and Mariah, and readied ourselves for a pleasant spring hike. Knowing that it was calving time for the moose, I planned to keep the dogs close and not let them wander off too far. One of the wonderful characteristics of German Shepherds is how their loyalty and desire to serve their people ensure that they never wander too far off. Unlike some other breeds, German Shepherds can be left off-leash in the outdoors. Tasha and Mariah always stayed fairly close to me. Nevertheless, I knew to keep them particularly close at this time of year with no wandering off into the bushes. We hiked through terrain consisting of gentle, rolling hills covered by brush, mostly comprised of alder growing about four feet high interspersed with the occasional black spruce tree, a hardy northern species that grows slowly and never seems to reach more than about seven feet tall.

We headed off with minimal emergency gear, suitable for a day hike in familiar territory. The only unusual incident was that something had prompted David to bring my 357 magnum handgun, given to me by my father. Now, I have to say that this gun was one of my prize possessions. Not because I love guns; I don't. I simply consider guns to be a useful tool, like a hammer, nothing more, nothing less. However, that gun represented a vote of confidence from my father, and his acknowledgement of my chosen lifestyle. His gift showed that he understood and accepted what my life was about, and it was therefore precious to me. David's bringing the gun along, which he wore in a hip holster, was not a usual practice for us. But he was listening to the still, quiet voice of intuition; and by doing so, he saved our lives.

We headed off on our trail, enjoying the beauty around us. Mariah, the more dominant of our two dogs, led the way, with Tasha trotting a few feet behind. We hiked through the hills, surrounded by a chorus of birdsong coming from the bushes beside the trail. We revelled in our freedom from the heavy coats we had worn all winter. As evening came, it was time to turn around and head for home. I had kept the dogs on the trail all day, and maintained a careful watch for moose. So far we had not seen any. We hiked back the way we had come. I relaxed my vigilance a little as we came back through territory we had passed a few hours before. As we paused to drink from our water bottles, Mariah wandered unnoticed off the trail and into the bushes. Suddenly we looked up to see Mariah running out of the brush with a cow moose hot on her tail. Now Mariah was a brave dog, and so she didn't lead her trouble back to us, but crossed the trail to disappear into the bushes on the other side. The cow moose, however, saw us standing there and swerved abruptly, changing her direction to gallop straight towards us. David frantically pulled his coat out of the way, got the gun out of the holster, and had just enough time to fire off a shot right over that moose's head. David was a consummate woodsman, and the very best companion with whom to explore the outdoors. Even so, it took a special act of courage, faith, and wisdom for him to fire over her head and not at her.

The moose turned abruptly in response to the deafening sound right above her ear. I will never forget the sight of her head wrenched to the side, one wild eye looking at me, as she swerved away from us. Knowing we were in trouble, Mariah came back to try and lure the moose off. The cow pursued her, and Mariah quickly escaped again into the bush. Our ordeal was not over yet. The cow turned again as soon as she lost sight of the dog and she again headed right back for us. All we could do was stand there. Again, David fired a shot right over her head, turning her at the last minute. Again, Mariah came back to try and lure the cow off. About that time, I looked down the trail in the opposite direction to see Tasha coming back. I knew that Tasha had neither the agility nor the speed to outrun a moose. With a mother's instincts I went to her, thereby leaving David's side and the protection of the gun. David yelled: "Get out of sight!", so I grabbed Tasha's collar and dragged her into the bushes. There was nowhere to take shelter, but as we crouched down the thick brush hid us from view. Mariah circled around and joined us. Now it was just David, standing alone on the trail. The moose charged him one last time; he fired off one last bullet over her head. David knew that if she charged a fourth time he would have to shoot her. My 357 pistol was a single action revolver. When carrying a gun in a hip holster, the firing mechanism should always be left on an empty chamber to prevent accidents. Therefore, my six-shooter only had five bullets in it, and there was no time to reload. No one with any sense shoots a moose with only one bullet available. That's why David knew that he would have to hit her with the fourth bullet if she charged again so that he would have a final bullet to finish her off if need be. Thankfully, Mama Moose gave up after the third charge. By then she was facing just one very noisy human. Having made her point by expressing her displeasure with our intrusion, she disappeared back into the brush. I am sure the whole interaction took less than three minutes, but these are three of the longest and most vividly remembered minutes of my life.

I will always admire David for having the courage, the wisdom, the self-control, and the pure woodsman skills to not shoot the moose on her first charge. You see, she was in the right, and we were in the wrong. As she trotted away, we could see the signs of afterbirth on her haunches. We knew she had one or possibly two newborn calves nearby which she was ferociously defending. My dog would not have hurt her babies. She was just curious, but the moose had no way of knowing that. The incident was entirely our fault for not keeping our dogs closer, and that moment of inattention could have cost us our lives. Angry moose have been known to stomp people to death, people who are unlucky enough to provoke them. A cow moose can weigh eight hundred pounds, and her sharp hooves are lethal. A moose can run thirty-five miles per hour for short sprints. There is no way a human will outrun a moose in open country. In fact, more people are hurt by moose than by bears in Alaska. This is an unknown fact to tourists, but something of which the locals are definitely aware. Every year the newspapers seem to carry at least one report of someone being killed in a similar, sudden encounter. This just goes to show that it is never a good idea to let down your guard in the Alaskan bush.

CHAPTER FIVE

BEAR COVE

AS WE BEGAN TO ACCUMULATE THE NECESSITIES OF LIFE AT our campsite in Bear Cove, it was time to graduate from our bucket to a real outhouse. David built one in town, and we brought it over with our boat. Now, the trick was how to bring our new outhouse up the steep bank to situate it over the hole we had dug. This was your standard-size, single-seat outhouse, and it was heavy. All we had were our two strong backs to get it off the boat and up the steep shoreline, a rise of about thirty feet. We tipped the outhouse onto my back with David taking the heavier, lower end and started to climb the steep bank, one small step at a time. The progress was slow as we inched up the hill, and more than once I found myself on my hands and knees with the outhouse propped against my back as David encouraged me from below. The absurdity of the situation eventually got to me, and I started to laugh. I was going to end my days squished by an outhouse! Pretty soon I was doubled over with laughter, still with the outhouse against my back, only now it was impossible to move. We both had a good, hearty laugh over the situation. Finally, my fit of laughter passed, I got my feet back under me, and we continued our gradual progress up the bank. Once we reached the flat area where our camp was situated, we were able to move the outhouse into place by placing logs underneath and rolling it. When our outhouse finally stood over the hole in the ground, we felt proud as new parents. We had really accomplished something! This marked the beginning of civilization in our little spot of paradise.

By cutting down trees on our property, we had expanded on a natural clearing in the woods. We now had a pile of logs accumulating which we hoped to eventually mill into lumber. I continually fed our burn barrel with discarded branches and we used a propane stove for cooking. We retired at night to the V berths in our boat. One day as I was resting quietly up in our campsite, I heard a soft noise. I looked down in time to see a small weasel scurrying through the underbrush, headed to our woodpile. This was a short-tailed weasel, a native species in the area, and a small but ferocious hunter. Darting into our

The Outhouse

woodpile, he emerged in a surprisingly short time with a fat field mouse which seemed almost half his size and more than half his weight. He had no trouble carrying it, however, and quickly dragged it off to wherever he made his nest. The bold little creature became a regular visitor in our camp, hunting the field mice in our woodpile. He wasn't too shy of us or the dogs, and I was always surprised at the speed with which he could capture a mouse and scurry off with his prize. Ounce for ounce he was probably the most fearsome predator in our territory, and as cute as he was, I was glad he was not any bigger.

The summer days were long and full of hard work. I was glad when evening came and we rested from our labors. We ate dinner by the light of our burn barrel before returning to the relative luxury of our boat. Inside our warm sleeping bags, we would stretch out on our V berths. There was just enough floor space for our dogs to lie down on the small rugs we provided, and thus all four of us would be cozy and dry for the night.

In the evenings I would sometimes hear the call of a great horned owl hunting in the branches overhead. Its distinctive, seven-note call seemed the cry of the forest itself: deep, mysterious, ancient. In the dark I would hear one fly through our clearing, tree top to tree top. The sensation wasn't so much a sound as it was a feeling: the waft of wind through his five-foot wing span, the down draft of air. They hunted the same mice that our short-tailed weasel did during the day. Mice, with their prolific breeding, are a staple for many predators including foxes, wolves, coyotes, and mink, in addition to our weasel. There is a hidden bounty in the forest of which the mice, who feed off the seeds and grasses, are an integral part. In this way, the circle of life is complete, as long as humans do not get in the way and spoil it.

The short-tailed weasel

Having an outhouse was an important first step, but now we really needed to complete our dock. David had traveled up to Bear Cove with a friend, eager to make progress on our building project. Completing the dock would make loading and unloading equipment and gear so much easier. Instead of having to muscle our loads up the steep hillside, we would be able to bring our boat right up to the dock at high tide and lift items up with a boom and a series of pulleys. David worked part-time for a barge company, and they had recently put a new deck on one of their ships. They were happy to deliver the old wood to our property. This scavenged wood, plus the pilings we had milled from trees, gave us the final ingredients we needed. After months of hard work the dock was finished with all the bells and whistles attached: rope tie-down spots, a sloping ramp up to our building site - the whole works. Our dock was quite an accomplishment, and David was proud. It had taken more than a year to get this far. After surveying his handiwork for a while, David decided that one of the neighboring trees was just too close; it posed a threat to his beautiful masterpiece. The tree had to go. David and his friend cleared the area where they planned to land the tree, and then David carefully cut a wedge in the trunk on the side he wanted it to fall. He then cut the trunk through from the opposite side. He sliced it through, but the tree remained standing. David and his friend looked on in horror as the tree swayed, and then proceeded to fall in the wrong direction - directly on our brand new dock.

As debris created by the falling tree drifted down around him, David looked at his shattered dock, speechless. His friend said: "Well, I guess all you could have done was run under it." This might have been tempting for David, considering the circumstances. Instead, after taking a few moments to adjust, David began the slow process of cutting up the obstinate tree, removing the broken boards from the dock, and rebuilding. This just goes to show how even the most carefully planned building project can experience "unexpected delays".

CHAPTER SIX

KAYAKING IN KACHEMAK BAY

SUMMERS IN ALASKA ARE FULL OF LONG DAYS AND SPECTAC-ular opportunities for those who love the outdoors. Even Anchorage, the biggest outpost of civilization, has the benefit of the wilderness only a thirty-minute drive away. In small towns such as Homer, the wilderness surrounds the small town, or strolls right in. Moose live side by side with humans and are a familiar sight. Cow moose have learned to give birth to their babies right in town in the front yards of residents to decrease the risk of predation by bears. One year, a cow moose left her calf by a bank's drive up window while she went off to forage. She had learned her baby would be safe there, and to the credit of Homer residents, everyone left the little one alone until Mama came back for him.

The beauty of the landscape is magnificent, and the five (usually) snow-free months from May to September provide unparalleled adventure opportunities for the outdoor enthusiast. Riding in our boat in the waters of Kachemak Bay gave us many encounters with wildlife. Multiple species of whales swim in the cold, clear waters of Alaska. In Kachemak Bay, the primary whale species are orca, grey, and humpback, most of whom migrate seasonally in and out of the area. Humpback whales come from their breeding and calving grounds around Hawaii to feed in the rich waters of Alaska. They are a common sight in Kachemak Bay in the summer time. David and I often spotted them while traveling in our boat. We were always careful to keep a long respectful distance to avoid disturbing their feeding. Sometimes, however, the whales made this very difficult.

On one occasion, from our boat David and I saw a group of humpback whales feeding in the bay a little way off in the distance. We shut off our engine and floated quietly as we watched. We were headed to Bear Cove, and we had a large fish tote on the deck of our boat full of gear. This was a plastic box about four feet square, and I stood on top to get a better view of the whales. As their feeding took them further and further away, we eventually decided to continue on our journey up the bay. David started the engine and put the boat into gear, while I remained standing on the box, high up in the air. Suddenly, right in front of our boat, we saw the back of a humpback whale as it rose up out of the depths. David slammed the engine into reverse and shut it off, and I was thrown to the deck. We watched in wonder as the huge tail passed beneath us, showing on both sides of the boat. I had narrowly escaped going overboard, which would have had me landing squarely on the back of that whale. Now that would have been an interesting experience, although not very pleasant for the whale or me in that frigid water.

While David and I got over our fright, the whale swam away. We continued on our journey. When we found ourselves nearing the whales again, we quickly shut off our engine. Our trip would be delayed, but these whales were a magnificent sight, and so we didn't really mind. While we waited, floating on the waves, one whale came up a few hundred yards away in a position called "spy hopping". This is a maneuver where a whale comes up head first, putting its eye above the water to take a look around. This whale was looking right at us, and we felt that it was keeping an eye on us, literally and figuratively speaking, to keep track of what the crazy humans were doing. We were very careful whenever we saw whales in the bay after that.

Another species of whale which frequent the waters of Kachemak Bay are the grey whales. These whales are not as prolific and they do not seem to hang out in groups, but they present their own navigational hazards. One day I was driving the Guinevere with a friend. As a commercial fisherwoman, my friend was supervising my boat-driving skills. Suddenly, she pointed and said: "Look out for that rock!" but then the "rock" slowly submerged itself below the waves before our eyes. The "rock" was the back of a grey whale. Due to their mottled appearance, they do look quite a lot like rocks. Afterwards I teased my friend mercilessly about the swimming rock she had pointed out to me. Truly, driving a boat is a tricky endeavor.

Kachemak Bay can be viewed intimately from the seat of a kayak; however, crossing from the Homer side to the far side of the bay is best done in a power boat. The tides can be fierce, and the weather can change drastically in fifteen minutes. With the weather transforming unexpectedly, several people have drowned trying to make the short crossing from the tip of the Homer Spit to the opposite side. For this reason, most kayakers use a water-taxi service to get to the other side of the bay. From there, by staying close to shore, one can kayak in relative safety while exploring the coves, inlets, and beaches of the bay.

Since David and I had our own boat, we would sometimes take a break from our labors and go kayaking. We had many memorable experiences on these various trips. I remember stopping on a beach to rest and stretch our legs. Suddenly, we saw a trio of river otters come up in the ocean, directly opposite us, where they began to call loudly. Both river otters and ocean otters live in Kachemak Bay. River otters bear their name because they frequently live in lakes and rivers, as well as the ocean, whereas ocean otters live exclusively in the ocean. River otters also come onto land daily, and live and breed in burrows close to the water's edge. They can move quite well on land. Ocean otters cannot move easily on land, so mothers raise their babies on their bellies. They float on their backs in the water until their young are old enough to swim. River otters, on the other hand, have multiple kits in burrows, and when the babies grow up they can be seen swimming together in small family groups of four to five animals.

David and I sat on the beach and wondered at the otters. They were obviously upset about something, as they were creating quite a fuss at the water's edge. Suddenly, on our left, another otter came running down the beach towards us, calling back to his family. When he saw us he stopped mid-call, as if to say "Oops", and quickly dove in the water. The family was reunited, and after some scolding, they all swam away together. Now, I do not know for certain who the players were in that drama, but it sure seemed like a mom coming to collect an errant teenager from lingering too long close to danger, the danger being us humans, of course. The family had seen us arrive, and had come to collect one of their members, who had perhaps not noticed us.

Kachemak Bay is full of ocean otters. I cannot remember ever taking a boat ride without seeing them, because they are everywhere. One particularly memorable otter experience happened just outside of Jakolof Bay, where David and I had been paddling in our kayak. As we emerged from the mouth of the bay, we encountered a kelp bed, and much to our surprise, we saw an ocean otter sleeping on his back. He had wrapped a few pieces of kelp around himself to provide a type of anchor while he slept. He didn't seem too concerned by us, though we had woke him up. He opened his eyes and watched us drift by in our kayak, but then he closed his eyes and went right back to sleep. Obviously this little guy had seen kayakers before, and he knew we were not a threat. I was able to take a couple of cute pictures of him sleeping there.

As we paddled on that day we saw many more otters, most of whom did not let us get that close. Sometimes we took them by surprise, however, when they came up from fishing on the ocean floor. They eat while swimming on their backs. One of their favorite foods is sea urchins, which they pick off the bottom and then bring to the surface to enjoy. More than once we were close to an otter as it came up, and I was amazed at the amount of noise they made while eating, kind of an enthusiastic: "Num, num, num" while munching happily on their catch. They are absolutely delightful creatures. Tour boat operators have to be careful when driving a boat through these waters as they are so prolific, particularly in the spring when female otters float with their babies on their bellies. The babies take time to learn how to swim at about four weeks of age. Their dense fur makes them too buoyant to dive until they get older, and so they live on their mother's milk, and ride on their mother's bellies. The females do not eat very regularly during this time. When a mother otter does need to eat, she wraps her baby in kelp to keep him bobbing on the surface until she returns.

Sleeping otter wrapped in kelp.

One summer David and I decided to take a longer kayaking trip into the headwaters of Kachemak Bay up to place called the Fox River flats. This area of the bay does not have a lot of boat traffic since the water is quite shallow. Still, it is accessible by kayak if one pays attention to the tides. Camping up there we saw a host of tracks in the sand near the water's edge: bear, fox, and coyote, possibly wolf.

We explored the shallower waters at that end of the bay. Our marine chart showed that in one cove a lagoon would form during low tides, with access to the main bay becoming almost impassable during these lows. A strong current runs through the main channel, coming in and out of this area with the tide. Paddling against this current is like paddling upriver. Although we had tried to plan our entry into this area, we had missed the optimum time. We only had a short window of opportunity to enter this lagoon. We paddled hard against the current, made it through the narrow neck, and gratefully rested in calm water after our exertions. Floating there, we admired the beautiful scenery of snowcapped mountains. The shoreline was covered in wild beach peas, their pink blossoms shining in the sun. After some time spent relaxing, we looked down, suddenly realizing that we had just a few inches of water left under our kayak. We were about to become stranded in a huge mud flat, where our only option would be to sit there for six hours until the water came back. Fortunately, by using our kayak paddles as poles, we were able with effort to pull ourselves into deeper water. We eventually made it to a steeper part of the shore where we could exit and drag our boat up the beach onto the rocks. Even the scenery in Alaska can be treacherous, as the sheer beauty causes one to stop paying attention. Our trip continued for several days, but eventually it was time to head back to responsibilities and deadlines. We paddled back the way we had come, planning to pick up our boat in Bear Cove where we had left it tethered to our mooring buoy. We had almost reached our destination. As we came around a small headland, we were surprised to see a boat that looked a lot like ours headed right for us. This was unusual. We hadn't seen many signs of humans for several days, and here we were running into a boat that looked just like ours. After a few minutes, as we got closer, we could not see any people on the boat. It took another couple of seconds for us to realize: my God, that is our boat. Somehow the Guinevere had come loose from her mooring and she was floating free on the tide, coming to meet us. How would we get from a kayak, where we were sitting a little below sea level, into a boat with rather steep sides? Our boat had high aluminum sides all the way around, and being a true Alaskan boat, she had no swim ladder. No one goes swimming in those icy waters. Eventually, David was able to climb up the outboard engine, and thus access the boat from the stern.

It was still a tricky operation, with me struggling to brace our double kayak and keep it steady while David clambered aboard the Guinevere. He started the engine and took her back where she belonged, while I followed behind in the kayak. Thank God we had hidden the keys in the boat, and didn't have them buried somewhere in our gear inside the kayak. We decided it was time to get a stronger line to tether our boat.

CHAPTER SEVEN

THE PROJECT IN BEAR COVE CONTINUES

AS SUMMER ENDED, WE CONTINUED TO WORK ON OUR LAND. We had started out trying to mill lumber with something called a chainsaw sawmill. This contraption could fit on a long-blade chainsaw, and as it cut horizontally it would slowly turn a downed tree into lumber. The process sounds good in theory, but it was slow going. We had used this chainsaw sawmill to cut some cross-beams for the dock. Once the dock was finished, David decided to build a bandsaw sawmill in town. We brought it out to Bear Cove. With a boom, a hoist made from come-a-longs, some rolling logs, and a whole lot of sweat, we finally got this sawmill set up on our property and ready for business. Now our time in Bear Cove was spent moving large logs with a peavey, another boom, and yet another come-a-long which we used to get logs into position so they could be turned into lumber on our sawmill. A peavey is a device which combines the leverage of a crowbar with a special hook to grab the log. The whole operation involves a whole lot of muscle, and the days were long, but now the sawmill was producing a wonderful pile of impressive lumber which we stacked carefully so it would dry straight. We would soon be able to start on our cabin.

David with large log, sawmill in the background

The snow came, and still we worked in Bear Cove every spare day we could find. There was no way we would have shelter this winter, but we hoped to start building the actual cabin in the spring. Our days were spent in hard work, and at night we retired to our little cabin on the boat. It was early winter in Alaska and we needed some heat. David installed a little gravity-fed oil heater on the boat in which the fuel oil slowly dripped into a pan where it burned. This was a very simple design which seemed to suit our purposes. Due to the cramped quarters in our little cabin, one of our dogs had to sleep right under the heater. She didn't seem to mind, and probably liked the heat. Our system worked well, except if a wind came up. Although the stove had a little chimney, too much wind would blow the flame out. Then the oil would continue to drip, forming a pool, which would eventually burst into flame as a result of the oil sitting on the hot pan. At this point, flames would begin shooting out of the stove, and our poor dog would have to jump up out of the way. David was eventually able to create enough of a wind break by using some form of a can on the top of the chimney. Even so, windy nights were not restful for any of us.

November came, and David and I decided to spend our four-day Thanksgiving holiday working in Bear Cove. We had a propane stove set up in our clearing under a tarp, and I had also learned to cook on the burn barrel. I precooked a turkey with stuffing inside and brought it out to Bear Cove where I finished cooking it on our propane stove in a Dutch oven. I prepared yams over the burn barrel. When we stopped working for the day, we enjoyed a real Thanksgiving feast, Alaskan style. David continued to run the sawmill, even though it had started to snow. This was hard, because the tracks upon which it moved had become covered with ice and snow. Still, he was a man driven, determined to have enough lumber to build a cabin in the spring. I took a picture of him pushing a massive log through the mill, covered in snow. I sent the photo to his mother with the caption, "Loretta, your son is crazy!" It takes a certain type of person to succeed in Alaska: one who is driven to move forward, despite all the obstacles that weather and Mother Nature can throw. David was such a person, and, yes, we did start to build the cabin in the spring.

David and sawmill in the snow.

David running sawmill in a snowstorm.

Camp cooking on Thanksgiving Day.

The dock and cabin frame from mooring spot with the tide out.

There were other cabins near our building site, but they were all deserted. In all the years we worked up there, we only saw other people once. So many people have dreams of life in the wilderness, but the impact of the total isolation is usually more than they bargain for. David and I heard one story of the people who had built on the property next to ours. Apparently a man had built the small cabin, and when he was finished he had moved his young family out there. When the man left for work, his wife stayed behind with their two young children. The weather turned, as it always does, transporting the woman and her children from mild summer to the storms and isolation of fall and winter. She was terrified, huddling in the small cabin with her children as a storm raged around them. She was not sure if they would survive. At the first opportunity she fled, never to return, and their cabin was abandoned. This is an all too common story in the North Country. Surrounded by civilization, we imagine the peace and quiet of the wilderness. Sometimes we can forget its implacable nature, and the harsh reality of being entirely alone. We humans rely on each other more than we realize. We take for granted the ability to make a phone call or ask a neighbor for help.

Most of the time David and I went to Bear Cove together to work on our land. A couple of times, however, he got someone else to go with him when I had to work. It really isn't safe to do wilderness construction alone, since in such a remote area a minor mishap can very quickly become much more serious. Therefore, going in pairs is always advisable. One memorable spring David was eager to go, despite inclement weather, but I was not able to get the time off. It was our practice to always listen to the marine weather forecast before heading out; however, we had also learned that while the forecast could tell us the big picture, it didn't give us the final say on whether or not we should make the trip. A final judgment had to be made at the last minute by going down and looking at the ocean. In this way we could determine if it was safe to travel the fourteen miles up the bay to Bear Cove in our little boat.

During the spring in question the winds had created some big waves on Kachemak Bay. David was anxious to get to Bear Cove, but the waves had been too big for safe travel. I knew that David's eagerness was tempting him to push the envelope of safety. He arranged to leave one morning, but had to cancel at the last minute - a very frustrating decision when the boat is loaded and ready to go. He decided to try again later in the day when the turning of the tide would bring the waves down a bit. Other mariners had taught us that if the seas were too rough to travel, you would often get a window of opportunity at the slack tide which comes in between the tide coming in and the tide turning to go out again. This short window, maybe forty-five minutes long, could sometimes provide a chance to travel for an otherwise stranded boater.

I knew David planned to "make a run for it" if the seas calmed down enough at the slack tide, and he promised to call me when he reached Bear Cove so I would know he had made it safely. I waited anxiously to hear of his safe arrival, but time passed, and he didn't call. After work I went down to the harbor, and the seas looked ferocious. He was gone, and I had not received word that he had made it safely to his destination. I agonized over what to do. Finally, as evening approached, I had to make a decision. As a search would not be possible once it got dark, I felt I had no choice but to call the Coast Guard. I knew it was possible that he had forgotten to call, but I had no way to reach him due to the mechanics of our phone reception. The phone only worked in carefully constructed circumstances. The possibility of his life being in danger was a risk I could not take. The Coast Guard said it was not a problem; they were in the area, and they would go and check on him.

David and his friend were eating supper when they noticed a helicopter using a spotlight to search the area. They were flying in a grid pattern, and David and his friend wondered what tragedy in the rough seas had precipitated the search. Suddenly, the Coast Guard shone its search light directly on them, and David's friend asked: "Did you remember to call your wife?" Oops! No, he had not.

The Coast Guard operator was pretty good about it, and said they were happy to help. He agreed I had been right to call, considering the alternative. Still, it was embarrassing for David and myself. The Coast Guard operator joked with me that David would probably never forget to call me again. Despite our embarrassment, I was glad the Coast Guard was there. David and I were not the type to rely on emergency services, but it was good to have a resource to turn to. I could not have asked any other small boat operator to go out on those seas to look for David. This was the only time we ever requested emergency services.

Traveling the bay in a small, flat-bottomed boat with only

a single engine when the waves are over six feet high is pretty nerve-wracking. This makes for a very rough ride. Perhaps more experienced mariners would have been less worried, or perhaps they would have avoided travel completely. We just didn't know. There is a saying about pilots which I think might apply to mariners as well: "There are old pilots, and there are bold pilots, but there are no old, bold pilots." There is simply no substitute for personal experience in the wilderness, especially when it comes to knowing where to set the limits.

CHAPTER EIGHT

TRAGEDY STRIKES

MY OLDER DOG, TASHA, HAD EVENTUALLY PASSED ON, AND David and I had adopted a new puppy. We named him Zeke, and from the size of his paws he was going to be a big boy. He quickly adapted to our lifestyle, enjoying the boat rides in our open skiff as we traveled up and down Kachemak Bay to and from our property. It was a wonderful life for a young dog. He had been born in the winter, and by May he was five months old and rapidly approaching the size of Mariah. Another purebred German Shepherd, he was a beautiful young dog with an expressive face and intelligent, brown eyes. He and Mariah roamed free on our property while we worked. They never strayed far. By then, our building project was well underway.

There had been some big wind storms that winter, and many more trees had blown down or broken off halfway up. Every time we came to the property we never knew what we would find. We had cleared most of the trees in the area of our campsite. But the trees in the area were all very tall, with some over one hundred feet, and there were still many that could hit our camp if they fell in the wrong direction. Whenever we were away we hoped for the safety of our outhouse and our sawmill, and so far we had been lucky. We were clearing the area as quickly as we could, but doing everything by hand meant that we could only go so fast.

One weekend in May, we came to the property particularly anxious because of a big storm that had blown through the area. We found several more trees down, but no damage. We checked the area of our campsite very carefully when we got there to make sure there were no "widow makers" lurking in the high branches. All seemed fine, and we settled in to work. It rained a steady Alaskan drizzle all day, so common for the region at that time of year. We got the burn barrel going, and I fed it branches from our logging project as well as debris that had fallen during the storm. We set up a tarp to provide shelter from the rain whenever we took a break from our labors. After a morning of hard work, David and I stopped for lunch. We sat under the tarp, the dogs at our feet. Zeke had stretched out next to the burn barrel, which was set up right at the edge of our tarp so that the smoke could escape but some warmth was provided in our shelter.

As we sat there peacefully eating our lunch, listening to the rain hitting our tarp, we noticed that a very slight wind had started up. With everything being so wet I was not concerned about the occasional spark from our burn barrel getting caught on the breeze. But suddenly there was a strange sound, a loud "crack". David looked out from under the tarp on one side, and I looked out from the other. We both saw the same thing: the trunk of a huge tree falling straight toward us. With no time to speak, we both dove out of the way. David dove in one direction, and I dove in another. Mariah, who always stayed very close to me, moved when I moved. The massive tree came crashing down right in the center of our tarp. Miraculously, Mariah and I were not hit. The branches of the tree, as thick as one of my legs, hit the ground all around us. By chance we were in a gap in the branches. I didn't know what had happened to David, whom I could not see at that time. I got gingerly to my feet, amazed that my dog and I seemed unhurt. Then I saw David, rising up on the other side of what was left of our tarp. Neither of us said a word; we just looked at each other with wide eyes, so stunned were we by what had just happened and the twist of fate that had left us both alive. Then we realized that Zeke had not been so lucky.

The main trunk of the tree had landed right on top of him. He never woke up from his nap; he was crushed instantly when the trunk, two feet in diameter at that point, fell on him.

We had to use the chainsaw to cut the tree off his broken body. I was glad to know that he had not suffered as he had been killed instantly. We grieved for our puppy whose young life was cut short. David was comforted to know that he had never known a moment of fear, but died as he had lived, free in the Alaskan wilderness. We buried Zeke's body in a small, natural cave just above the high tide line, and we used rocks from the shore to seal him in. Mariah was visibly shaken by the experience. She sniffed his body and watched us put him in his final resting place. The wilderness had claimed a life, but I had to wonder more at the miracle of our survival. Looking back, it was strange how the whole experience happened in silence, with neither David nor I saying a word. It showed me that our re-actions were quicker than our ability to form words from our thoughts. I was grateful for Mariah's habit of staying so close to me, and more than anything, I was grateful for the intuition that warned both David and me to investigate that loud "crack" coming from the tree canopy above.

Later we discovered that the tree which had fallen on our camp had been partially broken in the wind storm. It had a frac-ture in its trunk which had not been visible from our campsite.

Some other tree had fallen against it and broken it in the last big storm. In other words, the trunk was already badly damaged, and so it took just a slight wind to send the tree crashing down. We had been very lucky, and we had learned another lesson about surviving in the wilderness.

David with Mariah and Zeke (on the right) in Starlight Bay

CHAPTER NINE

GABRIEL HELPS US FINISH THE CABIN

AFTER ZEKE'S DEATH I DID NOT HAVE THE HEART TO RAISE another puppy. Their lives can be so fragile at the best of times, and our lifestyle was pretty rugged. Still, I knew I wanted another German Shepherd, and so I decided to contact a rescue organization in search of an adult dog.

I met several perfectly nice German Shepherds, but none of them touched my heart until I met Gabriel. I have learned over the years to listen to my heart when forming relationships, and when I do, things always work out beautifully. It is only when I use my mind rather than my heart that I seem to get into trouble. I met Gabriel when he was two years old. His young owner had a new baby, which had drastically changed her lifestyle, and so she was no longer able to care for Gabriel. He had been kept in a very small yard for the past year, and he was acting like an aggressive idiot when I first met him. Still, my heart spoke loudly and clearly that he was the one, and so I took him home with me. He turned out to be the most magnificent dog, and he remained very loyal to me throughout the remaining thirteen years of life. He loved the freedom I was able to give him by running on the beach in Homer and prowling around the woods in Bear Cove. Sometimes when David and I were working on our property and sleeping on the boat, we would put the dogs on shore in the early morning and go back to bed. Invariably I would soon hear "splish, splash, splish, splash" which would be the sound of Gabriel swimming laps around the boat, just to be close to me. He had a goofy personality, and he brought David and me a lot of joy. He made the loss of Zeke easier to bear, and he was a great companion in Bear Cove.

After five years of steady work, the little cabin in "Starlight Bay" was finally "finished", as much as a project like that is every, truly finished. The cabin measured ten feet by twenty feet, with a door, windows, insulation, and a woodstove. It was surrounded by a small deck. We were pretty proud of our little cabin, and we enjoyed finally resting from our labors. Our cabin was warm and snug, and it gave us a comfortable base to continue working on our land at a more relaxed pace. There was always something to do on our property. Just keeping the brush down was a lot of work! Still, knowing that we had a dry, warm, place to come home to made traveling up the Bay that much easier. We were free to follow other pursuits and continue exploring other parts of Alaska.

David and Jennifer with Mariah and Gabriel on deck of cabin.

The cabin finished

CHAPTER TEN

LIVING OFF THE LAND

ONE OF THE BENEFITS OF LIVING IN RURAL ALASKA IS THE ability to harvest resources directly from the land. In the Homer area there is a type of coal which washes up on local beaches in large chunks. Some people heat their homes with this coal. It has a higher sulfur content than commercial grade coal, but the price is right since it can be harvested for free from local beaches with the aid of a pickup truck and a strong back. It comes from coal seams which surround the bay, clearly visible on many hillsides. Storms and erosion break down these seams, and since the coal floats, it washes up in an abundant supply just like driftwood. In fact, early settlers called Homer "Smoky Bay", a reference to the smoke which resulted when some chance lightning ignited a coal seam or two, leaving them slowly smoldering. Modern residents long ago extinguished these slow burns and the atmosphere is now clear, but the affectionate name remains. There is also an abundance of driftwood on the beaches, but few people harvest this because the high salt content makes the wood a poor fuel. The coal is much more useful and provides a stable, slow burn in the right type of stove while leaving behind a distinctive, sulfur smell from the smoke. Many people also harvest wood to heat their homes from their own properties or from wood lots, where this is allowed. The Homer area has larger trees than many other parts of south central Alaska. Some locals supplement their income by harvesting wood and then selling it to their less physically active neighbors.

In addition to the free or relatively inexpensive fuel, there are many wild food sources. Large clam beds on both sides of Kachemak Bay are exposed about once per month by the extreme low tides common in the area. Razor clams, butter clams, and little neck clams (also known as steamers) are the favorites, and harvesting quotas allow you to harvest a year's worth of clam meat from only a couple of excursions. My favorites are the butter and little neck clams, which I harvested from the far side of Kachemak Bay. David and I would park our boat on the beach, tying it up to a log on an extreme low tide. Then, it was a race against the incoming tide to dig up as many clams as possible, storing them in five-gallon buckets full of sea water. This was a tricky maneuver which required constant attention to the placement of the boat. If we were not careful, we could easily become separated from our anchored boat by an expanse of icy water. The water in Kachemak Bay is so cold, even in summer, that I could not bear the pain of immersing my feet or hands in it for more than a few seconds. I would wear gum boots when clamming with the expectation of being covered in mud and fine, glacial silt by the end of a few hours of clamming. Little neck clams can be raked out of the gravel at a fairly shallow depth, but underneath these would be the larger butter clams, a real treat in clam chowder.

Once the incoming tide had chased us off the beach, we would rinse the clams in our five gallon buckets. When the water became clear, we would let them sit for a day in the salt water and give them time to expel all the sand from their bodies. Afterwards, it was time to cook the clams. I found that they could be frozen for up to a year out of the shell in the water in which they had been cooked, and thus I would always have a ready supply of clam chowder base waiting in the freezer. Locals do not harvest clams in any month with an "R" in it, which means May to August are the clamming months. This time frame is chosen to avoid the dangers of "red tide", otherwise known as paralytic shellfish poisoning, a natural toxin that can be found in clams at various times of the year. While the government periodically tests clam beds for this toxin, it is a localized phenomenon which can come and go, so people have learned to play it safe. I would be careful to eat only one or two clams from a batch, and then wait for half an hour or so. I would only do this when I was on the hospital side of the water, just in case. If I could eat one or two clams without my lips going numb, I would declare the batch safe to eat.

In addition to clams, vast amounts of Dungeness crab can be harvested in designated spots. Some people eat sea urchins, which are also plentiful, and a favorite of the otter population. The local waters teem with halibut, and Homer boasts itself as being "the halibut fishing capital of the world". Many tour-boat operators make their living taking hopeful fishermen out on the water, hoping to catch a big "barn-door" halibut, so-named because one fish can be the size of a barn door. It is not unknown for halibut caught in the Homer area to weigh over three hundred pounds. People just wanting to fill their freezers know that the little "chicken" halibut (twenty pounds or so) are much tastier, but tourists are enamored of the trophy-size halibut. Tourists who come to try their luck are affectionately known as "pukers", so-named because of the frequency of sea-sickness among them which is always an unexpected obstacle to a good day of fishing. Halibut fishing is particularly prone to inducing sea-sickness, since it is done while the boat sits on the anchor. The strong tides and currents in the bay often produce a washing machine effect with the boat sloshing around in all different directions. I took only one halibut fishing trip in the years I was there. I found that while I have no trouble with sea-sickness on a boat which is moving, I could not tolerate the chaotic motion of a boat sitting at anchor in the middle of the bay. Halfway through my halibut fishing trip, I was so miserable that I did not care about fishing; I did not care about the beautiful scenery. I was tempted to jump overboard, just to escape the constant, sloshing motion. Once we finally made it back to land after one of the most miserable days of my life, I swore off halibut fishing for good. I bought my halibut in the grocery store and was happy to pay the price.

The big tour boat operators, however, are readily supplied with new boatloads of unsuspecting victims every summer. When a big, barn-door halibut is caught, the guides have a unique way of advertising their success. Each captain carries a large caliber revolver on board, and when a really big halibut is caught, it is gaffed and then shot in the head before being brought on board. This safety measure is taken so that the huge, muscular fish do not take the boat apart when they flop around on deck. The sound of a gunshot is a form of advertisement. Other boatloads of tourists look on with envy wondering: "Which boat is that?"

"How big is the fish?" After a gunshot, the chatter on the VHF radio picks up dramatically.

Another local resource is of course salmon. Kachemak Bay has many natural salmon runs with fish coming to spawn up the nearby rivers and streams. The town of Homer has also created an artificial salmon resource on the Homer Spit, which is a seven-mile-long finger of land sticking out into the ocean. "The Fishing Hole" is a large artificial lagoon built with the aid of bulldozers. Once created, local fish hatcheries stocked The Fishing Hole with several species of salmon fry. Salmon return to the waters from which they are born, so by releasing the fry there, they have created reliable runs of salmon which return to The Fishing Hole. There is no stream up which the salmon can travel to spawn. Therefore, new fry have to be released every year. Still, the nice-sized fish which return make it all worthwhile. Tourists come from all over to park their motorhomes on the spit and fish in relative comfort on the banks of The Fishing Hole. Locals also come to fill their freezers with this bounty. The banks of this area can become quite crowded, but no one seems to mind. Of course, with so many anglers (some of them very inexperienced) standing around throwing large hooks about, there can be a few mishaps, but it is all enjoyed in the spirit of good fun.

Set-net fishing is another way of catching salmon which is

practiced by rural Alaskans. This is a method of net fishing from the beach to take advantage of the great tidal differential between high and low tides. Returning runs of salmon frequently swim very close to shore as they approach the mouth of the river up which they will spawn. A stake is put as far out as possible into the sea bed at low tide, and a net is strung, often on a pulley system, running horizontally towards the shoreline. When the tide comes back and the salmon approach the mouth of their stream, a portion of them are caught in this gill net. There is great excitement to be had watching the floats at the top of the net bob up and down as salmon hit the net. At the time when I was using this method of fishing, a householder with one additional resident was able to harvest thirty-five salmon per year by this method.

I did my set-net fishing outside the mouth of the Kasiloff River during the sockeye salmon run. These red salmon are particularly large and plentiful. I was able to catch my household quota in one day of fishing. This was a great harvest which filled my freezer and gave me enough salmon for the winter. I had a friend helping me with this fishing expedition, and her mother, a lovely Eskimo woman, showed me the proper way to gut and even fillet my salmon. She used an ulu, a traditional curved Eskimo knife with a big, flat blade. I was amazed at the speed with which this little Eskimo lady could gut and fillet a large salmon.

Seeing her experienced hands at work, I realized that an ulu really is the best tool for the job, when it is in the right hands. People who are set-net fishing frequently camp on the beach, since it takes at least twelve hours (the time between two low tides) to set and then retrieve one's net. This is a fun time, and people really celebrate when the fish come in.

Finally, one can also fish for salmon by dip-netting at selected times during the season. This is a method of fishing where you wade into the river, usually wearing chest-waders, and attempt to scoop salmon up with a hand-held net as they swim past. The nets are big; the poles are long; and a fair bit of strength is required to wrestle the salmon out of the current. Like other salmon-harvesting activities, this is a social event with families often camping on or near the beach as they wait for a run of salmon to hit the mouth of the river. On one occasion, David and I were dip-netting at the mouth of the Kasiloff River. He was standing in the current, chasing the fish with a net, while I stood on shore. A boat came in from the ocean and headed up the river, creating quite a wake. I looked down and saw a salmon at my feet which had been washed into the shallows. At first I tried to get David's attention to bring over the net, but he was already occupied, so I reached down with my bare hands and grabbed that salmon. When I triumphantly carried this salmon up the beach in my hands, I heard teasing calls from some onlookers: "Hey, no fair, you're supposed to use a net!" I knew it was just good-natured jesting, and I had no intention of letting go. Besides, I was quite proud of myself. I had a death grip on that salmon.

Another resource besides the bounty of the sea is the prolific abundance of berries growing on the hillsides in almost all parts of Alaska. Berry season is relatively short, but still a very important harvest for many people. Chief among berries is the ubiquitous blueberry. These are a favorite. Not only do humans harvest these berries, but bears do also, particularly grizzly bears. For this reason berry picking can be dangerous. It is important to pay attention and to keep a look-out for bears which can remain unseen as they prowl through the bushes. Bears, of course, get "first dibs" on any berry patch they choose. It is never wise to argue with a berry-picking bear.

CHAPTER ELEVEN

MOOSE

MOOSE ARE EVERYWHERE IN SOUTH-CENTRAL ALASKA. Anchorage, Alaska's biggest city, is built in a valley containing prime moose habitat, and so the conflicts between these huge ungulates and people are endless. Many moose are killed on the roads every year in Anchorage and on the highways heading north and south. So many are killed, in fact, that there are billboards warning people at key points on each highway with a death count kept every year. From July 1, 2012 to June 30, 2013 one hundred eighty-six moose were killed on the Kenai Peninsula Highway, which runs south from Anchorage to Homer. Not only are the moose killed in these accidents, but many people die as a result of these collisions.

The local human population has come up with a unique Alaskan way to deal with this carnage. This system might shock people who are not used to the practicality one is forced to develop when living in an extreme climate and in such a wild place. A list is kept in every locality where a large number of moose deaths occur. This is a list of people requesting access to roadkill meat. Many people, and even a few charity organizations, rely on this roadkill as a source of economical protein. Unfortunately the drivers who hit the moose are usually in no shape to harvest the moose meat at that time, and their vehicle is often incapacitated. When a moose is killed on a road, the person whose name is at the top of the list receives a phone call. They are told where and when the kill occurred, and they are asked how long it would take them to reach the kill and harvest the meat. If someone is ready and can go immediately, they are given rights to the meat. If they are not available, then the next person on the list is called. This practical solution feeds poor families and other enterprising individuals, and creates something good out of tragedy. As almost three hundred pounds of healthy, lean meat can be harvested from the average kill, this is truly a practical solution. Some families count on this resource every year to fill their freezers.

Driving the roads for twenty-seven years, I was extremely lucky to never hit a moose, but I did have a couple of very close calls. The first time, I was driving on the highway north of Anchorage, heading into the city. Just before dawn there was a steady flow of traffic on the highway. Suddenly, a large shadow passed in front of my vehicle. I didn't know what it was, so out of curiosity I tracked the shadow with my eyes. All of a sudden, I saw the car driving in the lane next to me fold up like an accordion. It was the strangest sight, and I will never forget it. Even so, I had not yet seen the moose. I pulled over to offer assistance, and it was then that I saw a huge bull moose with an enormous rack crumpled at the side of the road. He was still alive, but his legs were probably broken. The Alaska State Troopers would soon come by with a gun and shoot him; meanwhile, the occupants of the car crawled out of their wreckage, miraculously not severely injured. They were lucky that the moose they had hit was so large that he had not fallen on top of their vehicle, but rather stumbled to the side of the road. People are often crushed when they hit a moose at the top of its legs and the moose falls on their vehicle. In the car I had been driving which was much lower to the ground, the big bull would have likely fallen on me and I would have died before I ever knew what hit me, literally.

In another close call, I was making the five-hour drive from Homer to Anchorage to visit my mother. This was mid-winter, and there were high banks of snow on either side of the road. Since I drove this long stretch of road often, it was my custom to drive about five miles per hour over the speed limit (which was fifty-five miles per hour at that time) and thus shorten the amount of time I spent on the road. I had good studded snow tires on my vehicle, a four-wheel drive, and the roads were fairly clear. Still, as I approached a hill something told me to slow down. I have always been fairly intuitive and I have learned to listen to this soft, quiet voice from within. I reduced my speed as I went up the hill and around a corner. There at the top, I saw a large cow moose standing in the middle of the road. Time slowed down and some deep part of me seemed to take over the wheel. Somehow I steered around her and went "Poof" right into a snow bank. I passed so close to her rump that I could have leaned out the window and kissed it, if I hadn't been so preoccupied with saving our lives. I was grateful for the snow bank which stopped me, and after getting over my adrenaline rush, I was able to back out and continue on my journey. That was a very close call.

Moose have long legs for wading through the snow, but they still prefer the ease of travel offered by roads, driveways, and other areas humans have cleared. This often places them in conflict with humans. People have been stomped to death while walking to the end of their driveways to pick up the mail from their mailboxes. When the snow melts there are fewer conflicts, as the moose retreat somewhat. But they still come into developed areas, tempted by the tasty treats humans plant in their yards.

My mother, who lived in Anchorage, had an argument with one moose over her prize fuchsia flower-basket hanging just outside her door. She opened her front door one morning to get the newspaper, and there was a huge moose, munching away on her hanging basket. My mother was a courageous woman, and she didn't want to lose her beautiful flowers. She tried slamming her door, she tried yelling at the moose, and she tried other methods of making noise. Still, the eight-hundred-pound moose just looked on unperturbed, and ate that flower basket down to the roots. My mother was furious, but what could she do? A few days later, she stopped to get mail from her mailbox, which was a short distance from her driveway. She saw the same cow moose close by, lingering. Obviously, it had not yet eaten everyone's flowers. The moose saw my mother get out of her car and promptly charged her. The moose seemed to bear a grudge against the woman who had attempted to interrupt breakfast a few days before. That moose chased my mother around her car, but fortunately gave up once my mother hopped back inside. Moose that are really aggravated have been known to stomp cars, flattening them to the oil pan; however, that is extremely rare. Having made her point, the moose went back to eating the neighbor's flowers. It is a waste of time to argue with a hungry moose. They may be none too bright, but at eight hundred to one thousand pounds, they get what they want.

Moose in my mother's backyard.

In Homer, I remember the year one of my neighbors planted a lovely row of tulips right up next to the front of her house. I love tulips and was looking forward to the flowers opening. Unfortunately that never happened, because a moose came along one day and ate every one of those flower heads right off their stalks. It was a real shame, but it seems that moose like tulips, too. Moose also enjoy the various items found in a vegetable garden. One year I planted a long row of eighteen broccoli plants, hoping to stock my freezer with them. I watched happily as the plants grew and nice big heads of broccoli developed. When they looked just about perfect, I planned to harvest the next morning. Unfortunately, someone else had the same plan. I woke up to find every head of broccoli eaten. The moose had not left me a scrap, and only a few stubs remained above the ground. No other animal can do quite so much damage in so short a time. The same thing happened with my cauliflower crop, and my zucchini. It was most frustrating how the moose would wait until whatever I was growing was fully mature and at its prime, then come and decimate the whole lot. An eight-hundred-pound hungry herbivore can be very efficient. They don't nibble here and there like a deer or a rabbit. They come along and plow through the whole crop. By living in such a harsh environment, it seems that they have learned to be thorough when they find a food source. I eventually gave up on growing vegetables. I left this project to those who build eight-foot-high fences around their gardens over which they often string netting to cover the whole thing just in case a moose might try to jump the fence. On the other hand, I did notice that growing rhubarb is popular in Alaska. Moose don't like it.

Since having these immense animals lurking around town can be such a hazard to everyone involved, most municipalities have passed laws making it illegal to feed moose (I don't think trying to grow a garden counts). Before this law was passed in our area, or perhaps before it became widely known, it became evident that one of my neighbors was feeding a particular moose from the windows of his or her house. I came to realize this because some days when they were not home this moose could be seen going around the house looking in every window as if it was at a fast food joint, trying to see which drive up window was open. One day David and I had a fairly stupid idea. We decided to try our hand at feeding this moose, thinking it would be a great, photographic opportunity. We had a large flatbed trailer parked in our yard at the time, which proved to be very fortuitous. David approached the moose from about twenty yards and waved a carrot at her, trying to attract her attention. It worked! The moose saw the carrot and quickly headed in David's direction. David ran back to the trailer, hopped on top, and I got a couple of photographs of him feeding the moose. But when the carrots ran out, the moose was still hungry. She started to climb up on the trailer, and when David quickly jumped down off the opposite side, she began to chase David around it. We retreated to the safety of our house, amazed at the big animal's boldness. It became abundantly clear why it is illegal to feed a moose. It is about as smart as feeding a grizzly bear in your backyard: stupid, stupid, stupid!

*David showing the moose he did not have
any more carrots. She is not happy!*

I had many other encounters with moose in the years I lived in Alaska. I remember trying to teach my first German Shepherd, Justin, about moose. I thought I could teach him how to respond to them. At that time, I lived about a one-and-a-half-hour drive north of Anchorage in an area outside of Palmer. Since I lived on a large rural property covered with trees, moose were a familiar sight. I wanted my dog to learn to keep his distance, and to watch. I soon discovered my dog had more sense than I did. Seeing a moose on the property, I decided this was a teachable moment. I grabbed a firm hold on his collar and led him outside.

We approached to about twenty-five yards of the moose and I told my dog to sit. We calmly watched her as she foraged, but I guess she did not like the scrutiny. All of a sudden, she charged, and I turned and ran for the house. I had a firm grasp on my dog's collar, but he had slipped right out of it. Nevertheless, he was running right beside me, and we slipped into the house and slammed the door. Moose 1 point, Jennifer 0, lesson learned.

I had another memorable incident with moose when my dog Mariah was less than six months old. I lived at that time in a trailer in a very remote area next to a river. It was early winter, and moose, which are normally solitary animals, would sometimes congregate in small herds. I had let Mariah outside for her evening constitutional before going to bed. As soon as I let her out, she started barking ferociously. I looked outside to see a small herd of moose in my yard, consisting of a large bull and several cows. My puppy was right at the feet of this big bull, barking her little head off. I rushed outside, grabbed her collar, and hauled her away. The big bull just looked at us. I realized afterward that what I had done was not too smart. The bull could have easily killed me. But I was fortunate in the time of year: there was still a fair amount of food available, so the moose were not yet too grumpy. My puppy had decided to pick on the big bull, who was so large and so confident that he was not threatened by my dog or myself. Also, it had happened quickly, which was in my favor;

he did not have time to become too annoyed by the racket this small dog was making right at his feet. Instead, he seemed to be looking at her, trying to decide what he wanted to do. Mariah and I were both very lucky, and after that I learned to check the yard carefully before I let her outside.

I am not sure why moose, which are normally fairly solitary animals, sometimes congregate in small herds. It seems to happen in early winter, which may be related to the fall rut. It also happens briefly in the spring, right before the cows drop their calves. I believe this is a type of "predator flooding", which is a tactic used by other herbivores, especially in Africa, who have all their young at the same time in huge herds. Since predators simply cannot eat all the babies, many of them survive in this way. By grouping together, the cow moose perhaps give their babies a better chance of survival. Bears, which are predators of moose, are normally solitary animals, with the largest bear in an area having first access to food sources. By grouping together I believe only one mother in a group of moose will lose her baby to the resident bear.

At other times of the year moose are more dangerous. In February and March the moose are hungry, tired of the snow, and very irritable. That is a bad time to encounter a moose. Another particularly dangerous season is the middle of May when the calves are born, and finally the fall rut in September when moose have sex on their minds and the bulls are frisky. I had a memorable experience during the fall one early September in Denali National Park. The tundra was covered in crimson from the dark red leaves of low-bush cranberries, the wind was cool and crisp, and love was in the air. I stood on a hillside admiring the view of birch trees covered in golden leaves with a sea of crimson at their feet. Fall is a truly magnificent time of year to visit the park. As I surveyed the surrounding slopes, I saw a cow moose slowly walking across the tundra. Playing escort to her was an enormous bull moose with a huge rack, and what was most amazing was the way he was positively scampering around her. He cavorted around like a young colt, practically skipping. I could not believe that such a large animal could dance like that. She slowly sauntered towards some bushes where they soon disappeared, probably looking to continue their rendezvous away from prying eyes. His antics were a memorable sight.

Another time I was in the same park at the same time of year sitting around a campfire with some friends. All of a sudden we heard something large crashing through the brush, heading straight towards us. None of us knew what to do, and we scattered in different directions. I decided to move a few yards into a little clearing. I remember thinking that if something was going to attack me, I first wanted to see what it was. Suddenly, this cow moose rushed through our camp at full speed, narrowly missing our tent. She didn't even pause as she hurtled past, and I was glad to be out of her way. I never knew why she was running, but I know that moose are very excitable at that time of year. Perhaps a bear was chasing her, and she ran towards us humans as a form of protection, or perhaps it was the call of lust in her blood when she smelt a big bull in his prime nearby.

Getting run over by a frantic moose can happen in many different places. Perhaps they do use human campsites as a protection from bears. On one canoeing trip, David and I were camped on one side of a big lake while another group of campers were set up on the far side. As evening came, we heard a commotion. We looked up to see a cow moose plunge into the water, followed shortly thereafter by a young calf. Moose are strong swimmers from an early age, and both cow and calf made it safely to the other side of the lake. We continued to hear some commotion coming from that area. After about twenty minutes, three women who had been camped on the opposite side of the lake came paddling past in their canoe, their gear a tangled heap in the bottom of their boat. They explained that they had been sitting quietly around their campfire when suddenly a cow moose came charging into their camp and jumped in the lake, followed by her calf, followed by a bear. The bear broke off the chase when he encountered the humans, and so the moose's strategy worked. The three women had decided that this was too much excitement for their tastes, and they were headed back to their car. As I watched them paddle past, I had to admire the mother moose's ingenuity. Perhaps moose are not so stupid after all.

CHAPTER TWELVE

WHEN THE WINTER JUST WON'T END

LOVING THE WILDERNESS AS MUCH AS I DO, I HAVE TRIED TO share these experiences with friends on several occasions. On one such occasion, I took a friend on a kayaking trip in Kachemak Bay in early May. I expected a pleasant trip with favorable weather. Still, Alaska has taught me we don't always get what we plan for. It is always better to be prepared for the unexpected.

Since my friend and I did not have access to a boat at that time, we used a water taxi service to transport us to the far side of Kachemak Bay. We would explore the islands, inlets, and pristine beaches in this beautiful kayaking country. As we had planned for a short, three-day trip, we arranged for the water taxi service to pick us up on the evening of the third day at a specific rendezvous point.

The sun was shining on our first day as we explored the area, enjoying the unique, intimate view one can only achieve in a kayak. We observed the plentiful wildlife: otters, seals, eagles, and seabirds of many different species. The weather forecast had been reasonable and we were in fairly sheltered waters. We expected some rain on our second or third day and a little bit of wind with a moderate ocean swell coming in from more open waters. Still, as evening approached on our first day, the sky began to look a little ominous. We decided to set up camp on a protected beach just a few islands and inlets away from our rendezvous point. This turned out to be a very good decision.

We settled in for the night, well-prepared with our thick sleeping bags and winter long underwear, which we had brought along "just in case". The weather in Alaska is always unpredictable, and I have learned to always bring winter clothing no matter the time of year. We woke up in the morning to find snow on our tent, snow covering our campsite, and steady rolling waves crashing on the beach. Winter had decided to make another visit. It was May and should have been spring, but since I had already been snowed on in July in south central Alaska, I was not that surprised.

The waves told us to stay on the beach, so we prowled around our little area on foot while enjoying nature in her many disguises. We followed the tracks of a coyote which had apparently come to visit us in the night. I was grateful for the snow, because otherwise I would not have known of his visit. Still, I started to become a little concerned about our scheduled rendezvous with the water taxi the next day. I had failed to discuss contingency plans with them; what would they do if we did not show up at our rendezvous point? We did not have a marine radio with us, and we had no way to contact them. I was starting to realize these two omissions were a big mistake.

We settled into our tent for the second night. When we woke in the morning, we discovered a steady wind with four foot rollers crashing on our beach. More snow was falling. Now we had a choice to make: should we attempt to make it to our rendezvous point, or should we stay on the beach and hope that the water taxi would come looking for us? If they left us behind, would they come back? I knew better than to try and cross the bay in a kayak in any type of weather, so we were dependent on the water taxi to get us home. What to do? What to do?

We were both very experienced kayakers. We were in a double kayak, which is a very stable type of boat. We made the decision, which in retrospect may have been the wrong one, to launch our kayak and paddle over to our rendezvous beach. While watching the ocean we had noticed a slight break in the rollers caused by a submerged rock just off shore. We decided to launch, bow into the waves, and use this slight buffer to help us clear the beach. Still, it looked like we were going to get wet. We pushed off into the surf and paddled quickly past the shore break, meaning the point where the rolling waves curled before they crashed onto the beach. We had to paddle through this area without stopping to attach our spray skirts, so we both got a fair amount of water in our cockpits. Still, we made it through the surf without rolling and were then able to snap on our spray skirts and batten down the hatches, so to speak. We now faced an extended paddle in a driving snowstorm in four-foot ocean rollers. This was not a comfortable place to be. We had a fairly exposed crossing ahead as we headed for the shelter of an island directly in front of us. Once within the shelter of the island, we would be able to turn right and cross parallel to the waves towards yet another island upon which we had arranged to meet the water taxi.

I had never paddled in a snowstorm before, and I do not recommend it. I kept on thinking about the temperature of the water and the commonly discussed three minutes a person has if he or she falls in before the cold water sucks all ability to move. We paddled hard, and despite the rough ride, we eventually made it to the relative calm of the lee side of that island in front of us. We stopped for a few moments to rest and then carefully turned and headed to the beach of the next island over, which was our final destination. I was glad we were so prepared in our gear. We both wore heavy polypropylene underwear under waterproof clothes. Still, I was very relieved when we made it to our destination. We gladly went to shore, mopped the water out of our cockpits, and took off our waterproof clothes so that our specially designed under layer could dry off in the wind. By now the snow had stopped falling and the sun had come out, but there was still a stiff wind. We were happy to wait for whenever the water taxi might arrive. We watched the waves beyond our island. The size of the ocean rollers was steadily increasing in the unprotected water between us and the mainland.

The water taxi eventually arrived, and the driver seemed relieved to see us. He had a couple of other people aboard, and we chatted with them about our adventure. As we headed further out into the unprotected waters of the bay, the ocean swell grew in magnitude until we were riding in eight-foot rolling waves. We cut across them in a diagonal manner to head for the harbor. Our skipper was at first talkative, but he quickly began to ignore all conversation as he concentrated on the task of driving the boat. We were in a dual-hulled catamaran-style water taxi with two engines. As we saw him concentrating more and more, constantly adjusting the engines, we realized that our boat was in some kind of trouble. He was fighting to maintain control in the deep ocean swell. Being a good skipper, he made no comment to any of us on the boat, but applied all his skills to the task at hand.

We eventually made it safely back to the harbor. After unloading our gear, my friend and I stopped for a bite to eat at a small restaurant. After our meal, we came out of the restaurant only to see our water taxi on a trailer, heading away from the harbor, obviously in need of some fairly significant repairs. Yes indeed, the wilderness in Alaska is beautiful and pristine, and the opportunities for adventure are practically endless. Still, one needs to be properly prepared and to have developed contingency plans to avoid an Alaskan adventure turning into an Alaskan nightmare. I continued to be very lucky.

At the end of winter I was always eager for spring, which is my favorite time of year at any latitude, but particularly so up north. After months of darkness and cold, spring brings a renewal of energy. Leaves burst into color on the trees, and the animals become more active. Humans jump into action, tackling all the projects they could only think about during the cold, dark months.

David and I loved to go camping in the spring, particularly canoe camping, as it is a good method of getting away from people and the blemish of civilization into the heart of the wilderness. After one particularly long winter (though they all seemed long), we loaded the canoe on top of the four-wheel drive and headed off into the Swanson River drainage where there were many lakes and canoe trails just waiting to assist us in our escape. This is a lovely place with many interconnected lakes full of wildlife, and very few people.

We drove north from Homer for two hours to the town of Sterling, our jumping-off spot for the Swanson River Canoe Trails. From there we headed down the gravel road leading into the lake district until we came to the lake of our choice. Just one problem: it was still frozen solid. We realized then that in our eagerness we had jumped the gun on spring just a little bit. While the waters near Homer had thawed, our two-hour drive north had brought us back into the grips of winter. We were very disappointed, and as we sat in our car by the side of the road, we began to feel very foolish. Parking next to a frozen lake with a canoe on the top of one's car is embarrassing, to say the least. We felt like a couple of Cheechakoes, a term used to describe inexperienced newcomers to Alaska. What to do? Were the drivers of the few other cars on the road laughing at us? We imagined they were. We would be laughing if we saw someone else in this predicament. We reviewed our choices: 1) Make a run for home (this was not our style); 2) Use the canoe as a sled, and drag it across the ice (a definite possibility); or 3) Camp near the road, hiding the canoe in the bushes to preserve our dignity. We chose option number three.

We set up camp and began to explore. We had brought fishing

gear, of course, and I noticed that the edge of the lake, where a small stream entered it, was free of ice. I knew that ice fishing, where one drills a fishing hole through the ice of a frozen lake, was often a very productive venture. I thought I would try to at least catch us some dinner. I stood next to the open water and threw my baited hook in. Surely the fish would be hungry? Sadly, no interest was shown in my lure. I got close to the edge where I could see a good-sized trout down there, swimming slowly against the current. I dangled my hook right in front of his nose: no response. After trying this for a while, I became frustrated. Who did this fish think he was, ignoring my tasty treat? Eventually, I put the tip of my pole in the water and poked him in the side. He moved slowly away, and then just kept right on swimming leisurely against the current. Good grief! He was still so lethargic from the cold that he seemed to barely notice me. I realized I could use my net and scoop him right up, if I wanted to. I thought about this for a few minutes. Surely such a rude fish deserved to be eaten? Still, it didn't seem very sportsman-like, and I resisted the temptation.

I assessed our situation: First of all, we were camped too close to the road for my taste, though admittedly there were hardly any cars in the area. Our canoe was stashed in the bushes in a feeble attempt to hide our mistake: ("Oh sure, we always come up here before the lakes are thawed, don't you?"). Finally, we were going to miss out on our planned trout supper because the fish were ignoring my lure, leaving us with only pasta to fill our bellies. It was looking like it would definitely <u>not</u> be one of our best trips. Eventually, David and I managed to laugh at ourselves. We lived in the southernmost town on the Alaska road system, and our eagerness to get out into the woods had made us miscalculate, just a little bit. The lakes would probably be thawed in another two weeks. We would just have to wait.

As we left the Swanson River Canoe Trails a couple of days later with our canoe strapped to the top of our car, we waved and smiled at passing motorists who looked on with amusement. It was a Cheechako mistake, to be sure, or perhaps just a sign of a couple of old-timers beginning to lose their sanity after a long Alaskan winter.

CHAPTER THIRTEEN

SPRING

YOU CAN USUALLY COUNT ON SPRING WEATHER BY THE END of May, and I consider this to be one of the best times to go camping in south central Alaska. The bugs are not yet too thick, and are still dying off at night when it gets cold. The wildlife is active as they tend their young and fill their bellies after the relative hunger of the long winter months. David and I took many canoe trips into the Swanson River drainage at this time of year. On one such trip, we made our camp next to the shore of a lake. It was beautiful and serene, and though the lake was large, we had the whole place to ourselves. As we sat in camp eating the meal I had prepared over the open fire, we both began to be concerned about a noise we were hearing. After listening for a while, we spoke to each other about it. It sounded like a bird in distress. We decided to investigate, and soon spotted a baby bald eagle at the top of a large tree close to our camp. We scrambled through the brush to get closer to the tree and began to observe the young bird, trying to find out what was the matter. When I say he was a baby, I must clarify that he was the same size as a mature bald eagle, but he was still in the patchy plumage young bald eagles wear for their first few years of life. Sometimes people are confused by young bald eagles, thinking they are another type of eagle, because it can take four to five full years for bald eagles to develop their sleek adult appearance. Until then, they have a mottled look with white and brown feathers mixed together.

This young eagle was crying and carrying on. Was he injured? Was he somehow stuck on something? Since people go trout fishing in this area, we became concerned that he might have become tangled in some fishing line. Perhaps he had some fishing line caught on his foot, and was tangled in the tree top. We wondered what to do. He was about seventy feet straight up, but his cries tore at our hearts as he flopped around. Finally we could stand it no longer, and David decided he was going to try to climb the tree to see if we could help. We approached the base of the tree to figure out how this could be accomplished. As we looked up with concern from the base of the tree, the eagle looked down at us. After mutually regarding each other, he suddenly flopped over to another tree top. He was not stuck at all! All thoughts of climbing the tree were abandoned. He sure was acting pathetic though. He flapped his wings; he held them open at awkward angles; and he stumbled about on the branches making pitiful cries the whole time. As evening came we noticed a mature bald eagle show up with a fish. It did not land in the same tree as our baby eagle, however, but rather landed a few trees over. Ah, now we understood. This was a young eagle just leaving the nest and starting to fly. His parents were trying to encourage him by taking off for the day, but still caring for him by bringing him food at night. Still, Junior was going to have to fly a few feet to get his supper. He squawked; he cried; he flapped his wings; and he eventually flew the few feet required, making the most pitiful, awkward landing I have ever seen, wings all askew. He was rewarded with his fish, and the parent promptly flew away. It was like he was telling Mom or Dad: "I can't, I can't, I can't!", but they remained stoic and firm; it was time to grow up.

We watched the drama unfold over the next several days with both parents leaving Junior every morning, returning in the evening with supper, and staying nearby every night. He flew a little farther and farther every day, and by the time we left, his transition to adulthood seemed assured. I do not know if most baby eagles are this reluctant to learn to fly. Since he looked almost as large as his parents, it was hard to grasp that he was so very young. We think of eagles as such an emblem of freedom, independence, and majesty. Who knew they could be so insecure? I could not avoid thinking of the parallels to young humans, who also sometimes resist taking those steps to independence. Perhaps there is something humans can learn from eagle parenting skills? We should always encourage each other's independence and not buy in to limiting beliefs of weakness and helplessness. We humans of all ages are often like this baby eagle, afraid to embrace our potential. It was gratifying to see that with some gentle persuasion he would soon become master of the skies.

Not all camping trips involve drama. Some trips are so perfect they are practically idyllic. I shared one such trip with my Uncle Bryan. Bryan was my mother's brother, and I had not had much contact with him. To change this, he came up to Alaska to visit our family. David and I decided to take him on a canoe camping trip, since he professed a love of the outdoors. We decided to take him to one of our favorite lakes in the Swanson River drainage. We packed up and headed off. Bryan and I led the way in the big Coleman canoe with two German Shepherds and all of the camping gear, while David followed in his little single kayak. It was early June, the sun was shining, and new life was bursting out everywhere in the forest. Our destination was one lake removed from a popular canoe route. In this way we combined easy access and privacy.

Canoe camping.

We carried the canoe and kayak down a trail between two lakes and came out on Channel Lake, so named because the shoreline was irregular with many channels and inlets offering cozy places to camp. David and I returned to a spot we had used before. It was flat; there was a natural clearing in the trees; and to top it off, there was a very productive fishing spot on the shoreline right next to camp. We set up our two tents and created a comfortable camp. Since he was quite elderly, we had gone all out to make sure my uncle would be comfortable, even bringing a couple of soft, folding camp-chairs. The sun shone without a cloud in the sky. Despite the fact that it was already June, there were very few mosquitoes. I proceeded to fish, and quickly caught a beautiful Dolly Varden trout. Shortly thereafter I caught a lovely rainbow trout. I realized that I would soon have to stop fishing, since I didn't want to catch more fish than we could eat. I set up the pole and encouraged my uncle to take a turn. He did so, and after only a few minutes he caught another nice-sized Dolly Varden. He was pleased with his catch. We now had to stop fishing, since we had enough for supper. I do not normally catch and release, since the hungry trout usually swallow the salmon roe I use for bait and the hook goes in too far to be easily removed. I stored our fish on a stringer in the cool lake water to keep them fresh. I would wrap them in foil with a little butter and lemon pepper, and cook them in the coals of the campfire for our supper. Fresh trout are a tasty treat on a camping trip, and we would have one each, with maybe a few scraps for the dogs.

We decided to go for a paddle. As we cruised around the shores of the lake in our canoe, seeing what we could see, we came upon a cow moose eating by the water's edge, and behind her in the bushes we could see her adorable twin calves peeking out at us, curious about this strange apparition floating on the lake. We may have been the first humans these calves had ever seen, and the whole family seemed very relaxed and unconcerned by our presence. My dogs were used to the sight of moose, and so they just gently put their heads on the sides of the canoe and gazed at the moose family, flaring their nostrils as they drank in the scent. We continued around the lake, admiring the many species of ducks which made this lake their home. We saw bald eagles in the trees, obviously there to enjoy the good fishing, just like us.

When evening came we savored our succulent, fresh trout, cooked perfectly in the campfire. Since we had two different species of fish, we shared them to enjoy the contrasting flavors. Rainbow trout have white meat and the classic trout flavor, while Dolly Varden have a pink meat which tastes like a very mild salmon. With the evening the loons began to call, their haunting, eerie, cries the sound of the wilderness itself. We listened to quite an extended symphony that evening, and went to bed with the sounds of the wild echoing in our hearts.

Morning dawned clear and sunny. My uncle said he had passed a comfortable night, though I was concerned he might have been cold. He did not seem to have as much energy as I had anticipated. Still, he was in his early sixties, and so David and I were doing all of the paddling, lifting, and other camp work. That day we explored the hillsides around our camp, taking in the lush foliage and the multiple species of birds which had returned to the area. After returning to camp, we were visited by a muskrat cruising around the shore of the lake. He seemed unconcerned about us as he scurried around the water's edge, very close, while we silently watched.

Finally it was the day of our departure, so we packed up and headed back. When we got to the last portage, we paused to watch a group of loons fishing nearby. There were five, and they were doing something I have never seen loons do, neither before nor since. They were fishing co-operatively, which really astonished me, because loons are often very territorial. I had heard that loons will not normally tolerate other loons nearby, particularly in nesting season. Still, I saw what I saw, and it was remarkable. After lining up parallel to the shoreline, about twenty yards off shore, the loons swam in tandem towards shore, driving the fish into shallower waters. When they reached the shallows they dove, hunting the fish that now had less room to maneuver. Over and over they did this, while my uncle and I watched, fascinated. As they swam right towards the beach we were standing on, we had a chance to observe them closely. What a wonderful discovery to see these clearly intelligent birds working together like that!

Eventually it was time to head back to the car, and our amazing trip came to an end. Everything had been so perfect: good weather, few bugs, and lots of wildlife-viewing. It was like the whole trip had been choreographed just for my uncle's benefit. We took him back to Anchorage and dropped him off at my mother's house. They were scheduled to go on a glacier-viewing cruise in a couple of days out of the town of Seward. After we left, David and I talked about what an amazing trip it had been.

My mother and her brother enjoyed their day cruise where they witnessed the icy blue glaciers from the deck of their little pleasure boat. At the end of their trip, they spent the night at a hotel in Seward so that they could take their time on the drive back to Anchorage. Sadly, my uncle died peacefully from a massive heart attack in the hotel room that night.

When we heard the news, David and I were stunned. We thought about the possible ramifications. It had been less than a week since we took him camping. What would we have done if he had died on our camping trip? How would we have brought back his body? He was not a small man. How would we have carried him through the long portages? If we had left his body behind for the authorities to retrieve later, how would we have avoided his body becoming part of the food chain, considering all the bears in the area? Could we have strung him up in a tree? This whole train of thought seemed like something out of a bad Monty Python movie. It was macabre, to say the least.

Thankfully that did not happen. Instead, it seemed that

Mother Nature had blessed my outdoors-loving uncle with one last perfect camping trip. I can only hope that when I am older, and perhaps not able to get out on my own, someone will take me into the wild one last time and give me a trip like the one Mother Nature gave to Uncle Bryan.

CHAPTER FOURTEEN

THE MISSING LYNX AND OTHER MISSED PHOTOGRAPHIC OPPORTUNITIES

I HAVE HAD A MULTITUDE OF MAGICAL EXPERIENCES IN THE outdoors. Alaska is replete with wildlife which is there to enjoy if you slow down enough, watch, and listen. One time David and I were exploring the shores of a lake when we came upon a beaver lodge. While admiring its construction and wondering if there were currently any beavers in residence, we heard an unusual sound coming from the lodge. It sounded like a kitten softly mewing for its mother, or perhaps the sound of one nursing. We realized we were listening to the sound of a baby beaver. We crept away to avoid disturbing the young family.

I have also learned to pay attention to my dogs' subtle signals so as not to miss the quiet animals around me. My dogs' superior senses of smell and hearing have helped me notice many things I might have otherwise missed. Once, while sitting next to a campfire on the shore of a wilderness lake, Gabriel gave a low growl. I looked up to see a large black bear prowling along the opposite shoreline. He was on the other side of a little channel, about twenty-five yards away from me. Jet-black and in his prime, he was a magnificent specimen, his coat glistening in the sun. I was not sure if he was aware of us, so I just watched him quietly for a while. Finally, since he was headed around the lake in a direction which would quickly bring him to our camp, I decided to break a stick to let him know I was there. He glanced our way, but then continued on his slow amble. I didn't feel threatened by the magnificent bear, as he seemed calm and relaxed, just poking around looking for food on the shoreline. Since I was now sure he was aware of us, I trusted he would avoid our camp. Rather than continuing around the lake in my direction he started up the hillside, stopping to scratch his back on a tree. I watched as the tree top whipped back and forth. I couldn't see him anymore, but I knew what he was doing. I wondered if he would break the tree, so violent was its movement. After enjoying a good long scratch, he continued up the hillside. There have been many other times when my dogs have helped me notice a bear, a moose, or some other animal which I might otherwise have missed.

Sometimes wildlife announces itself. While camping on the shores of the Chena River near Fairbanks, I once heard the call of a lynx hunting on the other side. A lynx's call is unnerving, as it sounds like a cross between a human baby's cry and a cat's yowl. I have not heard this eerie and unusual sound often. Lynx are very elusive. In fact, a wildlife photographer told me that they usually joke among themselves about "the missing lynx", referring to the absence of photographs of this animal in most photographers' collections. I had one rare and amazing opportunity to photograph a lynx, but I too missed my shot.

Early one fall evening I was in Denali National Park with a friend, hiking down the gravel road which transects it. Since many animals are active in the evening, we hoped to get lucky and see some wildlife. We came to an area where a couple of gray jays were making quite a racket. They were calling loudly from above, moving tree-top to tree-top. I wanted to try and photograph these noisy birds, so I asked my friend to stand still while I balanced my camera on his shoulder. I used the zoom feature, trying to get a close-up of one of these birds. Then my friend said to me quietly: "Turn around." I did so, and there was a lynx, sauntering across the road much like a disgruntled house cat, while the birds continued to make a fuss about his presence. Now I understood why the birds were so agitated! My camera was set for a close up, and as I fiddled with it, the lynx finished crossing the road and disappeared into the brush. No photograph for me that day. Still, I have an image of that cat burned into my brain. What amazed me the most was how tall he was. He had long legs, like a Great Dane, and he truly reminded me of a house cat. He was trying to hold onto his dignity, acting like he didn't even hear the birds calling loudly as they flew from branch to branch. Yes, I now had my own experience with "the missing lynx".

Another iconic Alaskan animal which I have never been able to photograph is the wolf. They are very wary of humans, and despite seeing their tracks on numerous occasions, I have only ever had a clear view of one wolf. Driving north on the Parks Highway through a long stretch of nowhere, a wolf appeared on the roadside. He was chewing on a moose carcass, probably one that had been hit by a car and then stumbled off the road to die. By the time I realized what I had seen and turned around, he was gone. Darn! It would have been a perfect shot.

There have been other photographic opportunities that got away. On one of my earliest trips to Denali National Park, I arrived in early September. Travel on the park road is normally limited to tour buses and old school buses which the park uses to provide sightseeing opportunities for visitors. These buses run regularly in and out on the park road, about a five-hour trip one way. Visitors are allowed to get on and off the buses freely whenever they choose. In September, however, the road is opened to private vehicles, and I had driven to explore the park with a friend.

It was a beautiful sunny day, and after driving for a while I was anxious to get out of the car and hike. I decided to hike up the side of a mountain to enjoy the view from a higher elevation. I also - mistakenly - thought that if I hiked up to a rocky outcropping above the brush line, I would be above any bear activity. The mountainside I planned to climb ended in a rocky peak. I thought that there would be no chance of a bear wandering through at that elevation. I did not yet know how much grizzlies love the high country, but I was soon to find out.

I set out for my hike carrying my journal and a pen. I planned to sit safely on my rocky perch, enjoying the grand vista below me, as I documented my profound musings which would undoubtedly be inspired by the majesty of my surroundings. The crimson and gold colors of the park in September are truly magnificent. The summer rains were finally over, leaving a clear blue sky. My friend decided to wait for me at the car, as he wasn't too thrilled at the idea of hiking away from the road. Denali National Park is full of the stunning blond Toklat grizzlies common to the area. Still, as the park had never had an incident of a visitor being killed by a bear, I felt confident setting off on my hike. I had a plan, which I thought was a good one.

I hiked up the mountainside, being careful to avoid any brush-covered areas where I might surprise a bear. I stayed out on the open tundra. I had surveyed the area carefully before I set out, and hadn't seen any bears. I thought that from my high vantage point I would be able to see one coming from a mile away, and thus have time to hike back down to the car before it showed up.

It took me about twenty minutes to get to the rocky perch I had chosen. I settled in to admire the view, but... rats! I had dropped my pen somewhere during my climb. I debated with myself on the merits of going and looking for it. Did I really need to write in my journal? What was this compulsion I had developed to write things down? Wouldn't it be equally valuable to simply meditate in this spot without recording my thoughts for some future reading? I had convinced myself to stay, but then the voice of my responsible side began to lecture me: how could I think of leaving a pen on the tundra? I really should go and look for it. Drat!

I began my hike down the hillside, retracing my steps, looking for my pen. I left my journal waiting for me on my perch. I hiked all the way back to the car without finding my pen, so I decided to get another one and go back up. Then my friend pointed up to where I had left my journal. There was a grizzly bear, sniffing my notebook. Neither of us had seen him arrive, which means he must have been hiding in the one patch of brush I had hiked past. Now I had a dilemma. I did not want to leave my journal on the tundra for some future hiker to find; it had a lot of personal stuff in it. Plus, this was an even worse level of littering. I would have to hike back up and get it. I watched the bear thoroughly examine my notebook and the spot where I had been sitting, and then he climbed UP the hill to disappear over the mountain in the rocks above. So much for my theory that bears would not be hanging out in rocky areas.

After the bear disappeared, I hiked back up the hill and reclaimed my journal, keeping a wary eye on the rocks above. I no longer felt like meditating on that perch, so I headed back to the car. I was very glad the responsible side of me had won my internal argument; otherwise, I might have opened my eyes after meditating to find myself eye-to-eye with a grizzly. Not exactly the peace I was seeking; still, it would have been a great, photographic opportunity!

Some of the most beautiful sights in Alaska are elusive and transient, which perhaps makes them all the more sought-after and treasured. The tallest mountain in North America, Mt. McKinley, is also called Denali, meaning "The Great One" in the Athabaskan language. It is after this mountain that Denali National Park is named, as the park sits at the mountain's base.

The mountain seems to play a game of hide-and-seek with the photographers and tourists who come to catch a glimpse of its heights. Reaching a height of 20,237 feet at its summit, it creates its own weather, and is thus often surrounded by clouds even when the lower mountain range can be seen clearly. More than once, I have stopped at a rest area along the Parks highway only to see a carload of tourists peering at the mountain range, trying to determine which peak is Denali. I have approached these groups a couple of times, particularly on days when the mountain is peaking in and out of its own clouds, to direct the tourists' eyes upward, where they can catch a glimpse of the summit when the clouds disperse. I have told them: "Not down there, look up", and directed them to look at an area double the height of the surrounding mountain range. If Denali peeks out its head, I am rewarded by their gasps of wonder when the true summit is viewed. The sad truth is that the best time to view the mountain is in the winter, when clear, cold skies make the mountain visible even from Anchorage, over two hundred and fifty miles away. In the summer Denali is more often obscured by clouds. Unfortunately, the summer months are when most tourists, understandably, come to visit. They often have to content themselves with only a postcard of what they missed.

Denali

Another elusive wonder, also more easily viewed in the winter, is the Aurora Borealis, otherwise known as the Northern Lights. While I have seen the Northern Lights in the summer time, my most memorable viewings of this breathtaking phenomenon have been in winter, usually in the middle of the night. I am not sure why. Even though it gets dark early in the winter, still my most memorable views of the Northern Lights have occurred between two and five in the morning. For this reason, cabins with an outhouse carry their own secret blessing for those who wake up in the middle of the night.

At one point I had a volunteer job which required me to drive home through the broad expanse of the Matanuska Valley north of Anchorage about four-thirty in the morning. There were no street lights and no houses, just a huge, open valley surrounded by mountains. Many were the nights when I had to pull over and gaze in awestruck wonder at the display going on over my head. It was breathtaking and spellbinding. It is a good thing that I had these experiences before the advent of cell phones, otherwise I would have surely felt compelled to call people and wake them up so they could share in what I was seeing. The colors rippled and danced across the sky, sometimes shimmering like a moving curtain, sometimes coming together to form shapes directly overhead, only to quickly disperse again moments later. Sometimes the movement is swift, and sometimes the movement is slow, and while green and gray are by far the most common colors, I have also seen pink, purple, blue, and red. Coming home after a sometimes difficult shift at my volunteer job, this sight felt like a special reward for my efforts. With moon and stars illuminating the snow-covered mountain tops around me, and the Northern Lights dancing overhead, I would stand by the side of the road, tears streaming down my cheeks, spellbound in wonder by the stunning display above me. Eventually the cold would drive me back into my car and on my way home. In this manner, the North Country gets into one's blood, and despite cursing the cold, vowing to leave every spring, and refusing to endure one more winter, still people stay. It is hard to leave. The beauty and the majesty of the land are addictive. It is a pity that summer tourists often miss the best of it. Residents sometimes develop a bittersweet, love-hate relationship with the land, cursing the endless winter, but unable to move on to a more hospitable climate. The magic of the land takes root in their blood, like a drug or a bad love-affair, alternately cursed and cherished. For this reason, when long-term residents sell out and move south, those who stay behind often foretell: "You will be back." This turns out to be true, more often than not.

CHAPTER FIFTEEN

WILDLIFE ENCOUNTERS, BIG AND SMALL

IN MY YOUNGER YEARS WHEN IT WAS JUST ME AND MY DOG Tasha, I once took a long road trip up the Parks highway to Fairbanks, coming back in a big loop through Paxton. Tasha and I camped along the way, fishing the various rivers and lakes we encountered. I could usually catch enough fish to provide both of us with a tasty supper.

We stopped at the Chena River near the town of Fairbanks. The Chena runs fast, deep, and cold there, and is abundant with many species of fish. I decided to try my luck with a little fly-fishing. I am no expert at the art of fly-fishing, which is pure poetry in motion in experienced hands. But sometimes I had luck using an assortment of flies on my light spinning tackle, letting them float down the stream. Tasha watched as I dipped my flies in the swift-moving current. After observing for a while, she decided to start her own game while I played with the fish. There was a squirrel scolding us from a nearby tree, perhaps annoyed that we had camped in his territory. Now, every German Shepherd dog that I have ever owned has been crazy about squirrels. They seem to consider them a dangerous enemy, an aberration of nature. My canine companions take the job of protecting me from squirrels very seriously, pursuing the little creatures with vigilance whenever they are near. The squirrel and Tasha harassed each other back and forth while I let my flies drift down the river. Neither Tasha nor the squirrel seemed to have any intention of giving ground as they argued over the territory of my campsite. The squirrel was scolding us both, in the persistent way that only squirrels can, chattering loudly from the trees.

By evening Tasha found she had not yet chased off the little creature, so she decided to try a new tactic. I was lying down in my tent, reading a book with the door open. Tasha lay down on the ground by the side of my tent, hiding just out of sight. With both of us lying down, the squirrel eventually could not resist the temptation to investigate. He came down from his tree and scampered around. I watched his antics with amusement, and Tasha continued to lie still. I thought she had fallen asleep, and obviously the squirrel thought so too. He boldly grew closer and closer to me, when suddenly Tasha sprang out from behind the tent and chased the little guy right across the clearing. She had him right between her paws as she ran, but she never did try to bite him. She just gleefully chased him out of camp and back up his tree where he belonged. Very satisfied, she trotted back to me. I was glad she hadn't hurt the little guy and had only scared him. She had always been a gentle dog, and not particularly brave, but I guess she had finally found her match. She could protect me from that intruder, and boy, did she look proud of herself! Seeing her run with the squirrel right between her paws was hilarious. She taught him who was boss, and we endured no more scolding for the rest of our time there.

I tried my hand at fishing again later in the evening. It was summer, so the evenings were long. My efforts were finally rewarded by the catch of a lovely grayling trout. They are a small, beautiful fish, and look a lot like a miniature sailfish, minus the pointed spear on the front. I showed my prize to Tasha and she seemed suitably impressed. I wound up catching two grayling and cooked them in foil in the coals of my campfire: one for me, one for Tasha. I figured my mighty hunter deserved a reward for protecting me. She had chased off the dangerous intruder so we would be able to sleep in peace. This was a real victory. On another trip without my dog as companion I had experienced a squirrel purposefully dropping pine cones on my tent, preventing any chance of sleep, until I actually had to move my campsite. Squirrels can be very determined little creatures, but thanks to Tasha, that would not be our fate that night.

Sometimes, instead of me watching animals, I have become aware of animals watching me. At times I have been sure that they were laughing inside. One such incident happened in Denali National Park, where I had obtained a back country camping permit. Such permits are handed out sparsely and controlled carefully by the park rangers. The park has been divided into sections, and only a few campers are allowed to tent-camp in each section. It is also a requirement that back country travelers camp over one-and-a-half miles away from and out of sight of the road. In this way tourists and campers alike can trust that they will have a pure wilderness experience.

I had obtained one of these coveted back country permits. A friend and I took a rickety old school bus into the park, disembarking in the area for which we had a permit. We needed to be careful to keep our bearings, since the area right next to where we would be camping had been closed due to excessive bear activity. We were not sure what this meant, but it did not sound good. We started our hike. When we took our first rest stop, we happened to be standing on a tall hill, surrounded by the open tundra. The wind was blowing from our vantage point down into the valley below. My friend took out a small snack, which was - horrifyingly - a piece of smoked salmon, the scent of which was now wafting out into the surrounding area. I didn't know what else to do with this contraband, so we ate all of it and then washed our hands and faces with water from our water bottles. In my opinion, eating smoked salmon in grizzly country is not a wise choice, kind of like rubbing honey all over yourself and sitting on an ant hill. It was definitely time to put as much distance as possible between ourselves and this smell, so we headed off into a nearby river valley. We hiked down a stream bed and wound up setting up camp right next to this stream at the day's end. The next morning, I went to the stream to get water and lost my grip on the pot I was trying to fill. It quickly began to float down the swift moving current. I had to scramble over the rocks in a most undignified manner to try and retrieve it, which I was fortunately able to do. I collapsed to catch my breath after my efforts. When I finally looked up, I saw a herd of over a dozen Dall sheep on the opposite hillside. They were no more than twenty-five yards away, watching me intently. Was that a smirk I saw on a few faces? Just because they could traverse the steep, rocky slopes more gracefully than I was no reason to laugh at me. I stomped back to camp, chagrined.

Another place I like to go spring camping is on the south-facing side of a mountain where good drainage dries the ground out quickly and the southern exposure helps the hillside to thaw early in the spring. One year, David and I took one of these spring trips and camped on a hillside along the shores of Turnagain Arm outside of Anchorage. The steep, southern-facing slopes in this area are one of the first to be free of snow, and a favorite hangout spot for Dall sheep and other animals. The nights are still cold, however, when the sun goes down. We enjoyed campfires followed by retiring in our cozy tent. Tasha and Mariah accompanied us on these trips, and while they usually slept outside, sometimes on cold nights we would bring them into the tent where all four of us could enjoy the extra warmth generated by our combined bodies. I am not sure if this is true, but I have heard that Alaskan Native people sometimes would do the same, bringing a couple of their sled dogs into their shelters when it was particularly cold. Apparently the Rock & Roll band "Three Dog Night" named themselves after this practice, a "three-dog-night" being a particularly harsh one requiring the bodily warmth of three dogs, instead of just one or two.

On the trip in question we were all huddled together in our tent. My dogs seemed to be enjoying themselves as I lay squished between them. We had just settled in for the night when we began to hear a coyote barking and vocalizing in the distance. Mariah, my alpha dog who always took the role of my protector, answered, no doubt trying to warn him off. The only problem, however, was that it did not seem to be working. We heard the coyote growing closer and closer, with my dog growling and woofing at him. He would respond to her with his own barks and vocalizations. Closer and closer he came. We could only hear one coyote, so we were not feeling overly threatened by the situation, but what was he doing? Usually coyotes avoid humans, especially in Alaska where there is so much wild land and no reason for them to approach. But approaching he was, as he and Mariah exchanged a regular dialogue. It occurred to me that it was spring, and the single coyote was probably male. My dog was spayed, but I am sure she still had a female scent. Was he flirting with her? I have heard of coyotes mating with dogs, and I believe he was coming in because he had smelled her. I think he wanted to explore if she was in season. It was certainly the right time of year for this behavior.

We listened to their exchange for half an hour until it seemed he was right in our campsite. Finally, I decided it was time for all of us to get some rest. I called out: "Hey, some of us are trying to get some sleep here!" Their conversation stopped abruptly, and we heard no more out of him for the rest of the night. I am sure he crept away quickly now that he realized my dog had a chaperone. Her wild suitor was not going to get lucky this spring night.

There is a vast amount of unspoiled land in Alaska and countless places to explore. You could spend a lifetime exploring and still not see it all. One June David and I ventured farther afield to the large wild expanses of central Alaska, just off the road system. We drove into the middle of nowhere, parked the car by the side of the gravel road, and launched our canoe into a small stream. We were in a valley surrounded by steep mountains still topped by the last of the winter's snow. The air was a comfortable 60 °F; the sky was blue; the trees wore their mantle of beautiful green leaves once again; and the mosquitoes were hungry. Our dogs, happy to be out of the truck, looked on with excitement as we loaded the canoe. A couple of duffle bags, some paddles and fishing gear, and we were ready to go. The clouds looked like they might hold some rain, but if you wait for nice weather in Alaska, you will never go anywhere. The locals tell visitors: "If you don't like the weather, that's OK, just wait five minutes, and it will change." David and I had learned that on any summer camping trip we needed to bring heavy, thermal long-underwear, suntan lotion, shorts, and rain gear. The weather could change twenty degrees in a day, and we had better be prepared. There was no cell phone reception, and no one to help if we made a mistake.

The canoe was loaded with the dogs and gear, and we set off on another Alaskan wilderness adventure. Where else can you set off on an unnamed stream in an unnamed valley with no expectation of seeing another soul until you make it back to your car several days later? For David and me, this unchartered territory was our definition of paradise. The afternoon was spent in silence with only the buzz of mosquitoes and the chirping of birds for company. The brush closed in on either side of the stream, and we had to use our paddles as poles to push the canoe through the shallow places. It was peaceful, serene, and wild. We slowly slipped into a quiet meditative state, feeling the heartbeat of the land. Afternoon passed and we came to a hidden lake with a small group of trumpeter swans floating on the far side. We decided to look for a flat, dry spot on shore to set up camp for the night. Since it was summer, it was never going to get completely dark. But the sky looked like rain, and it was time to pitch our tent.

After setting up camp and having supper, we got ready for bed. It had started to rain, a light drizzle that was typical for summer. I wandered off a little way from camp to take care of evening necessities. While looking for a likely spot, I discovered an old moose kill, obviously the work of a bear. You can tell the difference between the sites where humans have killed a moose and where a kill has been made by a bear. Humans generally leave the hide on and take it with them, removing the offal. When a bear kills a moose, eventually all that is left is the hide; they eat everything else. I wasn't too worried by my discovery. The kill was old with only the hide visible, and I figured the bear had moved on. I found out later how very wrong I was.

I returned to camp and we settled in our tent with Tasha and Mariah sleeping outside. I will say right here that I am partial to German Shepherds, as they are a great breed to take into the woods. Their loyalty and devotion make them stay right in camp without ever having to be tied up. They are hardy enough to be comfortable sleeping outdoors, and a long lineage of police dog breeding gives them a fair amount of common sense. Nevertheless, my two girls had two very different personalities. Tasha was sweet, silly, and a bit of a coward, while Mariah always made it her job to set up watch. Any animal that came inside her established perimeter was going to get a warning, and she would let me know of its presence. In this way, I would be alerted to passing moose, porcupine, fox, or anyone else who wandered by. Knowing she was outside helped me sleep like a baby in the woods. I knew nothing would ever surprise me. From spending time with dogs, you come to develop an intuitive form of communication with them. You can tell a lot about what is going on by paying attention to your dog.

David and I crawled into the tent and into our sleeping bags, ready for a night's rest. A few minutes after we had stopped rustling around I heard Mariah growl, deep and low. I said to David: "That's a bear." We crawled back out of the tent. Keeping our backs to the lake, we peered into the brush with Mariah standing firmly in front of me. It was 11:30 at night, twilight at that time of the year in that latitude, and by watching my dog, we could follow the progress of a huge bear padding a semi-circle in the brush in front of us. Looking down, I saw our cook kit which I had washed after supper and set out to dry. I grabbed a pot and a cup and started banging them together while David stood beside me, pointing our 357 magnum handgun into the shadows, hoping the bear would not charge. Believe me: you do not want to shoot a grizzly of any size with a 357 magnum handgun. Getting shot would probably just piss him off, and he would eat us for his trouble. While this went on, Mariah continued to growl and woof at the bear, and at one point the bear kind of "huffed" back at her. After a few minutes of this stand-off, the bear withdrew, and my dog promptly went over, sniffed the path he had worn through the brush, and came trotting back with a sense of "All's clear." So David and I went back to bed.

A few minutes after settling back into our sleeping bags, Mariah started to growl again. It was beginning to look like it would be a long night. We crawled back out, beat on the pots and pans some more, Mariah had more conversations with the bear, and the bear eventually withdrew. Back into the sleeping bags we went, though I think by this time neither of us had much hope of sleeping. The bear came back once again. He wasn't going to give up. We were in his territory; we were camped in his spot; and he obviously did not like it.

To add insult to injury, the light drizzle had started again. While the bear circled in front of us, a beaver issued a warning from the lake behind us by slapping his tail on the water. I guess the ruckus we were causing was disturbing his sleep. The message we were getting was loud and clear: we didn't belong there. We had wandered too deep into the wilderness, and we had better leave. I said to David: "That's it, let's get out of here." We did something I have never done before or since: instead of nicely packing our gear, we just threw everything into the canoe helter-skelter and paddled away down that stream.

In case you are wondering where Tasha was during all of this drama, well, she was hiding under a bush. She ran out and jumped into the canoe, however, when she saw we had finally developed some sense and were leaving.

CHAPTER SIXTEEN

WINTER CAMPING

DESPITE MY PREFERENCE FOR SUMMER CAMPING, DAVID AND I have done some winter camping over the years, including one memorable trip to celebrate the New Year. This trip stands out in my memory because it was so very cold. We planned to ski in to a forest service cabin, where we would spend New Year's Day. We set off with the dogs and full backpacks containing all of our gear. Skiing with dogs, while wearing a forty-five pound backpack, is an interesting experience. It goes relatively well on flat ground, but going down hills can be treacherous. Having a pack on your back makes you top heavy, and there is the constant threat of tipping into a snow bank, if you are not careful. In addition, my dogs had the disconcerting habit of running down the trail in front of me and then suddenly stopping right in the middle of the trail, halfway down the hill, to look back up at me and see if I was following. This would lead to frantic yells on my part of "Move! Move!" My dogs would gaze at me affectionately as I hurtled towards them. More often than I care to admit, I purposefully wiped out in a snow bank to avoid crashing right into them. The added weight from the backpack already makes going downhill a bit of a controlled panic, and my dogs certainly didn't help.

It was a seven-mile trek into the cabin, which is a very reasonable distance for a skiing trip. At that time of the year the days are short, and even though we had headlamps, adding the dimension of darkness to skiing with a backpack and dogs was just too much of a potential disaster to contemplate. The weather was clear and cold, and the temperature just below 0 °F with a bright sun shining. We made it to our destination by late afternoon with the sun already below the horizon. We took stock of the cabin. It was really more of a hut, with no insulation and large visible gaps between the boards of the walls. The cabin had a small woodstove, and previous campers had left us just enough wood for us to get a small fire going. This is almost mandatory etiquette in the north. You never know what kind of shape the people who come after you will be in when they arrive, and the ability to make a fire can mean the difference between life and death in the north.

The little stove turned out to have a voracious appetite and didn't produce very much heat for all the wood we fed it. We would have to collect some more wood, and fast. The cabin had a very dull axe and an equally dull saw for collecting firewood. Fortunately, we had brought our own sharp, portable hand saw. We set off back down the trail. We had come through the remains of a small forest fire a while back, and so we hiked back along the trail to cut down one of these dry, dead trees which were still standing upright. David chopped down the tree with the axe, and we hauled it back to the cabin. We then took turns sawing the tree into sections to feed the woodstove. People say the nice thing about wood is it warms you twice: once when you cut it up, and once when you burn it. This is certainly true, and we developed a new respect for the pioneers of Alaska who heated their homes with wood before the advent of chainsaws. These people were a hardy breed. I remember a friend telling me about his grandparents. Every night after supper, the man and his wife would go outside and use a two-handled saw to cut up a day's worth of firewood. This was necessary to keep up the supply of wood. People truly lived lives of endless hard work back then.

Following in their footsteps, we cut up the tree and stacked the wood inside to dry. We were grateful to have found an old burn site, as this made the wood easier to cut and this wood was better for burning. With the stove cranked up we were able to take the chill off our shelter, but it was still in no way warm inside. By now the temperature outside was way below zero. The dogs slept on the bottom bunks and we slept on the top, and we enjoyed two days there. Though it was a memorable way to welcome in the New Year, staying warm took a lot of effort. The nights were clear and cold and the stars were bright. The light from the full moon reflected off the snow and so we did not need our headlamps to see. We did a little night skiing, just to enjoy the moon, but it was too cold to stay out long. We wore face masks, as any exposed skin felt the bite of winter quite sharply.

The day of our departure dawned clear and bright, and we packed up and headed out with the dogs trotting alongside us down the trail. I had a small thermometer with me that was designed for testing the temperature of the snow. This was an aid to help select the proper ski wax for cross-country skis. My thermometer said it was -5 °F in the sun. I noticed that whenever we stopped to rest along the trail, the dogs would pick up their feet one by one, trying to keep them warm. I had an insulated sleeping pad with me. Whenever we stopped I let my dogs stand on it, for which they seemed very grateful.

We made it back to the trail head. The car started (thank God), and so we headed back to civilization. Another successful trip, and a great adventure. We managed to save enough wood from our tree to leave the next people a nice little pile to get them started, but otherwise we burned the whole thing. The cabin never even became warm enough for us to take off all of our winter gear. Yes, indeed, I prefer summer camping.

Yet I was sometimes lured into other winter adventures by the enthusiasm of friends. Alaska attracts outdoorsmen of all different types. Some people want to escape the modern world; some people want to test themselves against the rigors of nature; and some people want to immerse themselves in the peace and beauty of the natural world. I am definitely a member of the third group. I like to enter the wilderness and just slow down, letting my mind, body, and spirit synchronize with the rhythms of the earth. Still, I knew many people who belonged to the other groups, and sometimes I would share adventures with them. I remember one such adventure when a group of us tried to traverse a glacier.

I had a friend who was very enthusiastic about glaciers, ice, and snow. He loved to challenge himself against the mountains and go off on thrilling expeditions as often as possible. I joined him and a couple of his other friends on one such experience. This was meant to be a four-day trip. We were going to ski across Eklutna Lake, which is north of Anchorage, climb up the face of the Eklutna glacier, cross the ice field flowing through the mountains, and come out at the other end. This was March, an early spring trip where we would have the benefits of longer days and some sunshine while we enjoyed our time on the snow and ice. My friend enjoyed working with ropes, harnesses, crampons, and ice axes. We were all carrying skis, but we started off wearing only our hiking boots. We also carried large backpacks full of extra warm clothes, sleeping bags, "skins" for our skis so they would grip the ice, first aid and toiletry supplies, food, water, snow shovels, ice axes, and other winter camping gear. We planned to camp out on the ice field for our second and third nights. Our goal for the first night was a forest service hut, perched on an outcropping of rock at the top of the climb. We would stop there after making our way up the face of the glacier, and then set out across the ice field.

We hitched a ride with some snow machine riders who gave us a lift across the long lake. This put us at the face of the glacier. We roped up and started our climb. The ropes were necessary because of the danger of hidden crevasses underneath the snow. We were a four-person rope team, with me in the third position. My friend was picking the trail, as he was the most experienced and thus the leader of our group. I was in the most protected position on the rope team because I was the least experienced of the group, and probably also because I was the only woman. We roped up and set off, picking through the visible crevasses as we tried to make our way up the face of the glacier. But we quickly ran into trouble. The snow looked solid, but due to temperatures being a little warmer than usual, it kept collapsing under our feet. This would often leave one of us dangling over a crevasse, held up only by the rope which connected us all together. We tried to walk across snow bridges between ridges of ice, but they were not as solid as they appeared. Sometimes our leader would make it across a patch of snow, only to have the second man fall in. Sometimes I was the unlucky soul; sometimes three of us would traverse a snow bridge safely, only to have the fourth man fall in behind me. This was a nerve-wracking experience. By keeping the rope taut we could prevent each other from falling very far, and we only fell up to our knees or our waists. Still, it is frightening to have one's feet dangling over a fissure in the ice, held up only by a rope and the strength and skill of the people around you.

There are two real dangers in this situation. First, there is the danger of the whole rope team falling in together; second, there is the possibility of one member falling far enough to become wedged in a crevasse, too tightly trapped to be pulled out. This is a very real scenario, and one member in our group told the story of someone he knew having to sit at the top of a crevasse, unable to dislodge his friend who was firmly wedged in the ice. He sat there and listened, unable to do anything, as his partner slowly froze to death in an icy grave. This was indeed a sobering scenario to think about.

After having made it up the face of the glacier, we continued trying to make our way across the ice field. With the growing dark it became too dangerous to try and pick a path, so we had to set up camp on the ice. We found a flat spot and set up our three-person tent. Our leader had brought a bivouac sack, and he was going to sleep outside of the tent directly on the ice in his sleeping bag. We used our skis and poles to probe the surrounding area, doing our best to make sure no crevasse lurked beneath, waiting to swallow all four of us in our sleep. We marked the inspected area carefully with upright skis to prevent any of us from stepping too far away from the tent and possibly into a crevasse. It was a very small circle. We made camp as best we could and waited out the night. I remember having to get up in the middle of the night to pee, and being afraid to take more than two steps away from the entrance of the tent. I am not sure if any of us got very much sleep.

Morning came and we packed up carefully. We put on our skis to give us a larger surface area for weight distribution and thus more protection from falling into a hole. It was a long day on the ice with each of us falling several times. The snow conditions were terrible, and we all knew we should not be out there. Still, once you are in the middle of a situation like that, there is nothing you can do but continue. We had put ourselves into this situation, and now we had to get ourselves out.

By the second night we made it to the forest service hut, high on the mountain. It was such a relief to feel solid rock under my feet, but the wind was howling and we were cold. We had a brief conference that night. It was obvious that we could not continue our trip, and would have to head back. The conditions were too dangerous. Now, the trick would be getting back in one piece. We would have to return the way we had come. I reflected a long time that night, and I came to the conclusion that as much as I loved the outdoors and my various adventures, I did not want to end my days wedged in the ice, slowly freezing to death. I made a bargain with God: if He would somehow get me off that glacier, I would never set foot on another one in my life.

Dawn came, and the sun shone brilliantly, glaringly bright against all that snow. Of course, the relatively warm weather was part of our problem, but at least the bright sky would help our leader pick out a trail. We gingerly made our way back over the ice field. We continued to fall through, but I guess we were all used to it by now. We were faster at pulling each other out and carrying on. We even got to use our harnesses a bit for the happier purpose of rappelling down a short ice face, which is a much speedier way of getting down a mountain. I knew the dangerous day was finally over when we reached the glacial moraine on the far side of the ice field, the side from which we had originally started. I realized I was probably going to survive this trip, and I found renewed energy to notice the world around me. The tracks of some creature were visible in the snow patches still lingering along the moraine. Due to the sunshine and the melting of the snow, it was hard for me to accurately determine the size of the tracks, but they seemed to be of a coyote or possibly even a wolf. I wondered at the animals that can traverse such terrain; I wondered if they ever had the misfortune to fall in a crevasse, or if their wild instincts somehow gave them an advantage we humans did not have. Maybe they were too smart to go out on the ice field in the first place; maybe they stayed on the relatively solid glacial moraine.

We reached the ice of Eklutna Lake. As the sun set, we skied across the smooth surface. It seemed that God had accepted my bargain, and death would find me on another day, in another form. I was very grateful. In all the years since that trip, I have never set foot on another glacier. It is not wise to forget a bargain you make with God.

Jennifer rappelling down glacier

CHAPTER SEVENTEEN

PORTRAITS WITH GRIZZLIES

OVER THE YEARS I WAS FORTUNATE TO EXPLORE VARIOUS places in Alaska. One such place was the huge and pristine Lake Aleknagik, the first in a chain of seven lakes in western Alaska in the Wood-Tikchik State Park. This park is about twenty miles by gravel road from the coastal fishing town of Dillingham. The series of lakes support fly-in fishermen and a couple of remote fishing lodges. These lakes are renowned for many fish species, including the five species of Pacific salmon, rainbow trout, grayling, Arctic char, Dolly Varden, and northern pike. The wildlife living off this bounty is abundant.

It was early June and the lakes were completely thawed. David was up at the park doing welding repairs on barges, and so I flew in to join him for a few days, and we took off on another wonderful wilderness adventure. He had arranged to borrow a collapsible kayak which we put together and loaded with our gear. Surrounded by low hills, we launched into the crystal clear water. Lush vegetation comes down to the water's edge all around this cold lake, and we soon spotted a grizzly on the shoreline eating the greens growing along the water's edge. When bears first wake up out of hibernation they cleanse their systems by eating these greens which are so plentiful at this time of year. We admired the bear from a safe distance as we floated on the water in our kayak. He ignored us and continued to feast. After a few moments of watching him quietly, we paddled on to continue our explorations. My plane had flown in at midday, and as it was approaching evening, we decided to make camp for the night. We found a sheltered spot on a little channel of the lake and set up camp. Walking along the water's edge, I stirred up movement in the reeds. Something huge and spooky was moving in the thick, floating vegetation. The reeds rippled and moved, hiding some unknown creature. I wondered, alligators? But it was too far north for that. I decided to slip a fishing line in with some bait to see what would happen. The water exploded with attack: northern pike, and hungry ones at that! They eat bugs, frogs, mice, or anything that might get too close to the water's edge. I tried for about an hour to catch one on my usual fishing tackle, but they kept breaking my line. Eventually, using a metal leader and a lure that looked like some kind of a frog, I landed one of the monsters. His teeth were sharp and plentiful, but the meat was wonderful and the taste of victory was sweet.

Later, while sitting around the campfire, we heard a noise. Something was prowling in the bushes nearby. David quickly jumped up and fired off a round from the shotgun we had brought along for the trip. He put the butt of the gun against the ground and fired it into the air to save wear and tear on his shoulder. The loud boom was eventually followed by silence, and as twilight descended, we crawled into our sleeping bags for a deep, restful sleep in the fresh air. We had scared away our visitor, for now.

Morning came, and we quickly rose and broke camp, eager to get on with our day. We paddled out of our little channel and continued to explore the big lake. Soon we spotted another grizzly on the shore, munching on greens like the first. A little further on, we saw yet another grizzly. Pretty soon we realized the shoreline was littered with them, every quarter mile or so. Our unknown visitor of the previous evening now seemed a bit more ominous. We agreed that from now on we would stop on one of the many islands that were scattered throughout the lake whenever we set up camp. While we knew that all bears are competent and strong swimmers, we hoped that by camping on islands the bears would not accidentally step on us as they approached the shoreline for their daily greens. You never want to get between a bear and a food source.

We continued our paddle in the bright sunshine, seeing bears everywhere. I got the crazy idea that this would be a great opportunity to photograph bears, even though all I had with me was a cheap, Instamatic camera which miniaturized everything. I asked David to paddle close to the shore so I could photograph a bear at the salad bar. David cautioned me that we shouldn't get too close, and he prepared to paddle away if it charged. Looking back, I realize I wouldn't want to test my paddling skills against a grizzly's speed. But at the time, all I could think of was the wonderful photographic opportunity.

Having taken my fill of candid bear shots, I decided it was time for David and me to take each other's portraits in the kayak with a grizzly in the background for good measure. Thus followed a series of portraits, with David grumbling the whole time that this was not too smart. Fortunately, the bears were more interested in their greens than they were in us, and we got away with our pictures, unscathed. I have always regretted not taking a better camera on that trip. There would have been some world class shots. Unfortunately, all I have to remember the day are a series of snapshots taken with an Instamatic, which I like to call my "portraits with grizzlies".

The second night we camped on an island. I was glad we had the shotgun along just in case, but without my dogs standing watch I was still a little nervous. Fortunately, the night passed uneventfully. We woke up to another glorious day on the shore of this cold, clear lake. David decided to do some fishing to supplement our usual oatmeal for breakfast, and he quickly caught a nice pink salmon.

Now, after so many years in Alaska, I admit that I have become something of a salmon snob. There are five main species of Pacific salmon: king, otherwise known as chinook; reds, also called sockeye; silver, called coho; pinks, otherwise known as humpbacks; and finally chum salmon, also referred to as dog salmon, because the native people of Alaska feed this species to their sled dogs. My preferences were red, followed by chinook, then silver. I normally would not eat pink salmon, even though this is the species commonly used for the canned salmon available in stores. I found the meat mushy, and as an admitted salmon snob I preferred the rich flavor of sockeye. Still, fresh fish is a wonderful treat on a camping trip, especially compared to the bland fare we brought with us. When camping in bear country, which is pretty much everywhere in Alaska, David and I would live on oatmeal and pasta with dried fruit, nuts, and cheese for lunches. We were always careful to pack low-scent foods so as not to lure trouble to our campsites. No bacon and eggs for us.

That is like putting out a welcome mat for all the bears in a five-mile radius.

We started a fire, wrapped the fish in foil with a little bit of lemon pepper, and cooked the fish on the coals. What a feast! When that fish came out of the fire it was the most amazing pink salmon I had ever eaten: moist and succulent with the flesh still fairly firm. Nothing like the pink salmon I usually rejected. We had a wonderful breakfast and ate as much as our stomachs would hold; still, there was quite a bit left. Now the question arose, what to do with the leftovers? Neither of us was very keen about walking or paddling in the area while carrying bear bait. Still, it is wrong to waste food. We wound up burning the foil we had used for cooking in the campfire until it was a blackened lump smelling mostly of soot, and then we packaged the remaining meat in plastic bags. We packed out all of our garbage, of course, stowing it in the bow of the kayak until we were back in civilization. We finished the pink salmon at lunchtime, and we fed what was left to the fish. Neither of us wanted to make camp in grizzly territory with anything tastier than dry oatmeal and dry pasta nearby. Even so, we always hung our food bag in a tree and washed ourselves and all cooking utensils carefully before bed. For the rest of the trip we made a habit of fishing for breakfast or lunch, cooking our catch on a fire, and then paddling away from our cooking fire with all of its yummy smells before we made camp for the night. The bears in the area were busy feasting on spring greens, but I didn't want to tempt them to move on to the main course, particularly not in my camp.

CHAPTER EIGHTEEN

PRINCE WILLIAM SOUND

MOST OF ALASKA IS WILD, PRISTINE, AND FREE, BUT NOT ALL of it. Perhaps the greatest environmental tragedy to ever happen in North America was the Exxon Valdez oil spill on March 24, 1989. A huge oil tanker, the Exxon Valdez, hit Bligh Reef, and the resulting rupture to its hull spilled an estimated 41.5 million liters of crude oil into the once-pristine waters of Prince William Sound. Residents of Alaska, former visitors, and nature lovers from all over the world reeled from the enormity of this environmental disaster. While some made their fortune by quickly enlisting their boats and other resources in the clean-up efforts, many people, including whole communities, lost their livelihoods, their homes, and their way of life as a result of the long-term impact of this catastrophe. After years of concentrated clean-up efforts and billions of dollars thrown at the problem, the oil companies and some governments said that the problem had been contained, the harmful effects had been mitigated, and environmental harmony had been restored to Prince William Sound. I am here to tell you I do not believe this to be true, as I found that ecosystem still devastated by the oil spill many years afterwards. I discovered this when I went on a five-day kayaking trip in 1999, ten years after the spill.

David and I had enjoyed many kayaking trips in Kachemak Bay. One year we decided to explore Prince William Sound, since it was also famed to be beautiful, and reports were that all traces of the devastating oil spill were long since gone. We started our trip in Whittier, a secluded town nestled against the base of the surrounding mountains. Whittier has a population of only 190 residents, due in part to its limited employment opportunities, its isolation from the road system, and its reputation for terrible weather. Still, the beauty of the surrounding mountains and glaciers are well-renowned, and the tiny town is a key transit point for travelers. Many tourists take short boat trips from Whittier to see the famous Columbia Glacier, a tidal glacier which ends right on the ocean, calving huge ice-bergs into the sea. To be sure, it is awesome to witness the huge chunks of ice slough off, creating a mighty boom as they hit the ocean.

Prince William Sound

The area near Columbia Glacier is not a safe place for kayaking, since these huge floating icebergs can roll suddenly when their lower portions melt sufficiently in the sea water and they become top-heavy. These sudden corrections of balance can be disastrous for those who get too close, so tour-boat operators and kayakers must keep a safe distance between themselves and the floating icebergs. David and I, therefore, steered clear of the glacier. We were more interested in the wildlife anyway, which we hoped to enjoy amid the spectacular scenery of the sound.

Being used to the teeming waters of Kachemak Bay, I quickly noticed the contrasting silent beauty of these waters and shores.

We did not see the usual host of otters, eagles, sea birds, and shore birds that we were used to. We kayaked and camped there for many days, and the beaches, mountains, and tributary rivers were beautiful. But where was the wildlife? We did not see tracks of animals on the shoreline; we did not entertain curious visitors of all shapes and sizes. There was an absence of birds; the lovely land was curiously empty.

I realized now the importance of organizations like Cook Inlet Keeper and other environmental monitoring groups. These groups attempt to inventory wildlife in healthy ecosystems. Without taking count of the various species of wildlife before a disaster occurs, how can we really measure the devastation that lingers long after the visible signs of an oil spill have been cleaned up? We had no such numbers to compare. There was no measurable data with which to confront the oil companies and hold them to account. People kept track of the animals and birds which were rescued, cleaned of the foul oil covering their bodies, and subsequently released, but did they survive? When the food sources, and in fact the whole ecosystem has crashed, what can these animals live on? What diseases or nutritional deficiencies made them later die and drift slowly beneath the waters of the Sound, never to be seen again? There was no count, so no one knows. But I am here to tell you the waters of Prince William Sound were still mostly dead, ten years after the clean-up of the Exxon Valdez oil spill. The recovery efforts were labeled a "success" by those who never really had to account for what happened. It could happen again, if we are not careful, and if we do not hold the oil companies to higher standards (which would mean less profit). Surely the lives of the inhabitants of an entire ecosystem are worth more than the obscene profits enjoyed by those who are made rich by the oil industry. Let's hope we do not have to repeat this terrible lesson in order to learn what we must.

CHAPTER NINETEEN

VALLEYS AND RIVERS

DURING MY FIRST YEARS IN ALASKA I LIVED FOR A TIME IN the Matanuska Valley, north of Anchorage. For seven years I lived on a large piece of property in the hills outside of Palmer. The valley is home to some of the original homesteaders who were lured to Alaska by the government with the promise of free land. The Homestead Act was signed into law in 1862 by President Lincoln, however it was not until 1898 that is was extended to include the territory of Alaska. The deal was that if a family could clear and farm a given area of land, build a house on it, and then live there for at least five years, then they would be given title to their land. In this way the government drew forth the bold, the brave, and the desperate to homestead and colonize the forty-ninth state. Only the strongest, hardiest souls survived, raising their families on land they had cleared with the sweat of their brows. Those who were weak or less than determined either perished or crawled back home to the lower forty-eight states. The families who remained were resilient stock, and their descendants live on in the Matanuska Valley and other rural areas of Alaska. It was a privilege to mingle with these hardy souls during my time there. Parts of the Matanuska Valley, particularly those parts where the tall mountains keep the land in perpetual shade, can see temperatures of - 50 °F in the winter where paying attention to survival is a necessity of life. I learned to never set out in my car without winter survival gear in stow. In addition to winter boots, a heavy coat, and a shovel for digging out of snowbanks, many people also keep a winter sleeping bag in their cars. In case of accident, injury, a car breakdown, or sliding off the road, a good sleeping bag can mean the difference between survival and death while waiting for rescue. This is truly a land where the fittest - or the most prepared - survive. Still, nature seems to like variety, and random exceptions do occur, perhaps as nature's way of experimenting with different possibilities. Chance brought one of these random variations to my doorstep in the form of a miniature Bull Moose.

It was early winter, and a fall wind storm had blown down many trees on my two-and-a-half acre property on the top of Lazy Mountain. Most of the downed trees were birch, and while my partner and I slowly cut the trunks into firewood and stacked them, the area around our cabin became littered with the tops and branches of these trees which turned out to be prime moose food. This bounty resulted in an almost constant parade of moose through our yard, often travelling in groups of five to six animals. Among this number came an individual the likes of which I have never seen before or since. He was a perfectly formed miniature Bull Moose, no bigger than a fall calf, less than one-half the size of the cows. Everything about him was in proportion including his rack, which looked normal, but was sized to suit his body. Although he was hanging out with a group of cows, he would have had no chance to breed in the fall rut, his small size making the mechanics of the situation quite impossible. Still, the cows seemed quite comfortable with his presence, and I observed them together for several days. It was early winter, approaching the time when Bull Moose shed their racks to grow them anew in the spring. I realized what a prize his miniature rack would be. The person on the neighboring property who had also seen the little bull said he was watching for it too. Neither of us got lucky, however, and eventually the group of cows moved on, followed by the little bull. I have never even seen a picture of such an animal, and unfortunately I did not think to photograph him myself. This just goes to show that despite all the talk of survival of the fittest, nature also likes to give variety a chance. Luck also plays her part in who dies and who survives.

Wild rivers course through the many valleys in Alaska, and fishing is a popular sport for tourists. One of the most popular of these rivers is the Kenai, which runs wide, deep, and cold through the Kenai Peninsula. The water is a milky, light blue color, common in the big rivers in Alaska which have their headwaters fed by glaciers high up in the mountains. The color comes from the fine glacial silt in the water, a powdery substance made of pulverized rock that is created when a glacier creeps down a mountainside or flows through a valley. The substance, which is familiar to anyone who spends time in the North Country, has a tendency to permeate everything. The wind swirls it around anywhere in the proximity of a glacier or a glacier-fed river which means pretty much everywhere in Alaska. Despite its milky appearance, the water of the Kenai River is pure, cold, and full of many species of fish including rainbow trout, steelhead, Dolly Varden, and salmon. Huge schools of these salmon migrate up the Kenai River each year, heading back to the tributary streams where they were born. The mighty Kenai supports runs of four species of salmon from early summer to late fall, but the most impressive and popular with anglers is the spring run of king salmon, also called chinook. These fish are giants; the largest ever caught in the Kenai River was ninety-seven pounds. They are a coveted prize for sportsmen who come from all over the world to try their luck in these waters. One year I took a fishing trip with my older brother, Michael, a guided float trip down the Kenai River, to see if we could get lucky.

We started out on the river in a small boat which the guide maneuvered with a pair of oars and a strong back. We had paid for an all-day float trip to give us plenty of time to catch our dream fish. King salmon can be finicky, and they aren't really feeding when they hit the fresh water. Most times they hit the lure out of aggression and a territorial drive. In other words, the real hope is to piss one off so much that it strikes your lure. As my brother and I started out on our trip, the guide sampled various lures and tackle to try and attract the attention of a big king salmon. Due to the cloudy water, the fish aren't visible. Since they come and go up the river based on tides, water temperature, and the whim of their spawning instincts, an angler just has to hope that they are down there lurking in the murky depths.

It was a sunny day and a relaxing trip with our guide doing all of the work. All we had to do was hold our poles, drift along, and enjoy relaxed conversation. For quite some time there was no activity on our fishing lines, which was fine, because this gave my brother and me a chance to catch up on the news in each other's lives. Like I said, salmon are fickle creatures, and we were fishing blind. Luck is a definite factor in whether or not a prize is brought home from a salmon fishing trip.

Our guide continued to change our tackle, trying to provoke a strike. After about an hour-and-a-half, BOOM! - my brother's pole bent. "Fish on!" our guide cried. He expertly maneuvered the boat away from the bank to avoid giving the fish a chance to tangle and break the line in the vegetation growing alongside the river. Michael had his hands full, because this big king salmon was fighting. It was obviously fresh from the ocean, having come up the river with the incoming tide. It was a thrill watching my brother's pole bend as he struggled to land his fish. King salmon don't normally jump; instead, they roll like a crocodile, using the weight of their bodies to fight the hook. Michael was eventually able to tire out his fish. He brought it alongside the boat, where I used a net to scoop it up. This was the biggest freshwater fish ever caught by either my brother or myself: a twenty-five pound beauty! Our trip was a triumph, and we still had many hours remaining to see if I might also get lucky.

The rest of the day passed peacefully, floating leisurely down the river. Our guide continued to change our tackle and steer the boat to all his favorite fishing holes, but my line was being ignored by the fish. It looked like I might get "skunked" and have to content myself with the thrill of my brother's catch. Getting "skunked" means not catching anything. This is always a very real possibility when fishing, particularly when fishing for salmon. But it didn't really matter; it had been a beautiful day. The end of our trip was in sight in the form of a dock, which signaled our final destination.

Suddenly, my pole bent in half, nearly touching the water. Our guide sprang into action by maneuvering the boat and giving me instructions. Whatever had hit my line was now towing us upriver! I was fishing with a twenty-five pound test line, but this thing seemed way bigger than that. The guide used our boat and the current to help me fight this fish. It was a monster! After about half an hour, my arms were aching with the strain, but there was no way I was going to give up and let anyone help me with this fish. I was in for the fight of my life. I let the fish run upstream, and when he turned, I tried to reel him back in. It was a constant battle, back and forth. Over and over he took my line, over and over I fought to get it back and bring him closer. We hadn't seen any sign of him, but we were sure it was a king salmon because of its size. He was staying deep and away from our boat. Finally, after an hour, he came close enough to the surface so that we could see him roll. Oh, my God! I almost dropped my pole. I couldn't believe the size of him. It looked like he could easily swamp our boat, if he tried.

I continued to fight that fish with the help of our guide. After an hour-and-a-half, the salmon and I were both exhausted.

Our guide steered the boat towards shore because there was no way we were bringing a fish that size aboard. Eventually, I was able to land the fish on shore with the help of a net, and we finally got a good look at it. I had caught a sixty-five pound king salmon! We found out it wasn't a he, it was a she, and she was full of eggs. She was starting to turn pink, and she was sporting a second lure. She was literally "the one that got away" from someone else. I caught her on a green Spin 'N' Glow lure, which I of course kept for posterity. I thought it was interesting that the other lure she had struck was also a Spin 'N' Glow, but that one was orange. Now she was mine; it was indeed my lucky day.

That fish was almost as long as I was tall, and I got a year's worth of salmon for the freezer from her. I also froze her roe and used it for bait for many years to come. There is nothing better for rainbow trout or Dolly Varden fishing than untreated salmon roe. I learned that if I spread some on a log and let it dry in the sun for a while, then it would stay on my hook long enough to catch trout.

The long day of fishing had surpassed my wildest dreams. When I brought that fish home, I needed help carrying it inside. It took up the whole kitchen counter top, and I had to borrow room in someone else's freezer to store it all. My cats had come to investigate the smell of fish, but they were visibly terrified when they saw her stretched out in the kitchen. Yes, this had been a truly unforgettable day of fishing.

Jennifer with 65 lb king salmon

CHAPTER TWENTY

TERMINATION DUST

MANY ALASKANS HAVE A LOVE/HATE RELATIONSHIP WITH snow. In fact, developing feelings of dread around the arrival of snow is a sure sign that one is destined to leave the North Country, and probably soon. I myself became one of these people. I remember the year I found myself shoveling the snow off of my front lawn after a late April snowstorm. It always seems to snow in April - a cruel trick of Mother Nature, to be sure. In Homer, the winter snow has often melted by then at the lower elevations, and I anxiously awaited the first green shoots of spring. But invariably every year, a big storm would dump a huge load of snow on our town, just when the more optimistic (or desperate) of us thought our ordeal was over. When I found myself shoveling the snow from my lawn, like some deranged maniac with a tenuous grasp on reality, I realized my days in the North were numbered. It was time to find somewhere warmer to live where I could indulge my fondness for gardening and other warm-weather pursuits. To add insult to injury, on the day I was shoveling my lawn one of my neighbors walked down the road with his young son, and I heard the child exclaim: "Look, Daddy, that's the house where the monsters live." The child was referring to my celebration of Halloween the previous October, when I had put on quite a display with sound effects and everything to playfully terrorize the neighborhood children. Still, as I shoveled my lawn like a crazy woman, I thought the child was not too wrong. I had become like a woman possessed, desperate to see something green out my front window, instead of the everlasting white and grey of winter.

Postcards and other pictures show heartwarming images of cozy cabins covered in a white blanket of snow. There is usually a fire glowing warmly, visible through the frost-rimmed windows. Rosy-cheeked people smile happily from these pictures, making snowmen or enjoying other prosaic pastimes. These images are a blatant lie. Let me tell you what it is really like.

In addition to my regular job, I had started a pet-sitting business as a way of making some extra money, and perhaps also as a way of meeting other animal-loving people such as myself.

People from Homer often take trips to somewhere warm in the winter, and they need someone to take care of their pets. I had taken care of everything from the usual dogs and cats, to a group of seven horses, to a five-foot long iguana named Bud. Most of these animals I took care of in their own homes, which meant I needed to travel all over the area no matter the weather. I had a good four-wheel drive vehicle with studded snow tires and a long history of driving in winter conditions. I was as prepared as one could be. Still, my last winter in Homer provided some memorable driving experiences.

I had agreed to take care of two golden retrievers from a new subdivision in town. The roads in and out of this area were still gravel, which is not unusual. I had agreed to visit the dogs twice per day to let them out, feed them, and spend some time with them. It was late December, and their owner would be gone for a couple of weeks. The weather had been typical for that region. While the snow began in October, in true coastal fashion the temperature had gone up and down, alternately thawing and then freezing again. This meant that the ground was frozen hard and was covered in ice. On top of this ice there was frequently a thin layer of water whenever the temperature rose above the freezing point. The roads were thus a skating rink, and some days it was just best to stay home. Due to my pet-sitting responsibilities, however, I could not stay home. The animals were counting on me, and I would not let them down.

On Christmas Day I set out to take care of the two golden retrievers. The gravel road to their home was a sheet of ice with a small hill leading up to their driveway. I put my car in four-wheel drive and made a run at the hill, but the water atop the ice combined with the slight grade proved too much for my vehicle, and I slid off the road and into the ditch. Oh, well, now I would have to walk up to the house. I made it up the hill by hiking through the snow at the side of the road, and I took care of the dogs. Now I had to get home and find a way to get my car out of the ditch. I began the long hike home, my legs making post holes in the snow, sinking up to my thighs. I could have used some snow shoes, but alas, I had not thought to keep a pair in my car. After all, I was still within the town limits. My biggest problem arose when I had to cross over other driveways, as these were all icy and covered with water. I had two choices: hike around the house and driveway through the snow, or somehow get across the slippery surface. I found that if I sat down on the ice, I could push off from the edges of the driveways, and if I gave it enough force, I could slide across the ice to the other side on the seat of my pants where I would be stopped by the snow on the far side. To me this seemed to be the only safe way to cross these patches of ice, since standing up was impossible. In this way I slowly made my way home. It took a long time, but I made it. I was grateful that I never went anywhere without proper winter clothing, but I realized I had not been fully prepared. I had neglected to bring crampons and an ice axe, which would have helped immeasurably. Most people do not think to pack these when they are only driving a couple of miles across town.

Yes indeed, it was time for me to seriously think about leaving the North Country. People who have come to feel the way I do refer to snow as "termination dust". In fact, a large group of people spend only their summers in Alaska. They arrive shortly before the tourists and leave shortly after them. We call them "snow birds". In panic they regard the slow progression of the snow line coming down the mountainside, and they always head south before it hits town. Others head south, never to return, except for short visits. When I began to discuss my plans to leave with friends and acquaintances, I was often told: "You'll be back." Many believe that after spending too long in the North Country, one is ruined for a more civilized environment. This is often true, but still, that final winter made me think I would give leaving a try. The "termination dust" had finally gotten to me.

CHAPTER TWENTY-ONE

TIME TO SAY GOODBYE

BEING BORN AND RAISED IN CANADA FOR THE FIRST TEN years of my life, I had always felt a calling to return to the land of my birth. Meeting David had delayed those plans, but when the frozen North started to get to me, and the pull of a more temperate climate became too strong to resist, I knew it was time to go. I spoke to David about my feelings. He was happy as a clam in his life, but I had reached the realization that I just could not go on with what I was doing. David and I still cared for each other deeply, but I think he realized that it was time to let me go. I loved the wilderness of Alaska, and the unparalleled opportunities for adventure, but I had found that I had begun counting on my fingers the months that I loved in Alaska, compared to the months that I endured. I kept coming up with the same numbers. There were five months that I loved: May through September. But there were seven months which I endured: October through April. These turned out to be all the snow-covered months. I realized that I was a person who loved to walk, and I was living in a land where even the moose sometimes fell down on the ice. As I took stock of what I loved to do, I found that three of them were activities that were severely limited by the weather where I lived. I loved to garden, I loved to swim outdoors, and I loved to walk on unfrozen ground. In parallel with these realizations, I knew that certain areas in my life seemed to have come to the end of their natural life cycle.

I had been working as the local drug and alcohol counselor for eleven years in Homer, a town which was made famous by a bumper sticker which read: "Homer, a quaint drinking village with a fishing problem". This bumper sticker of course referred to the struggles of our local commercial fishing fleet, coupled with the off season activity of many fisherman. I was on a first name basis with most of the town's alcoholics and problem drinkers. Alaska has a legal system whereby those who get arrested for driving while intoxicated have a choice: serve thirty days in jail, or go and get some drug and alcohol counseling. It is easy to imagine how working in such a court ordered system made me popular in my small town. Still, over the years

I seemed to have earned a grudging respect from some of the worst offenders. They would call me up saying: "Jennifer, this is John (or Bill, or Steve or whoever), I got in trouble again". After a while even without a last name I would recognize their voices. I began to wonder if I had been doing my job for too long. Maybe some fresh talent was in order. It was hard watching my friends die of alcoholism, in all the various, tragic, and creative ways an alcoholic can die in the North Country. I just couldn't do it anymore.

My relationship with David also seemed to have come to the natural end of its life cycle. In my life I have learned that sometimes good relationships come to an end. One spiritual source I have studied likens relationships to a fine banquet. Just because the meal ends, it does not mean that it was not good. My relationship with David had come to a fork in the road. It was time for both of us to move on in different directions to continue our lives. I gave David the property at Starlight Bay, our cabin, and the Guinevere. He had put in the most effort, and it seemed only fair. David still lives in Homer. He bought a cabin fifteen miles out of town, on the road system this time. Of course, being a builder, he expanded his cabin, and it continues to be a "work in progress", with absolutely breathtaking views of Kachemak Bay, right outside his front door.

I eventually sold our house in town. Then I headed off down

the Alaska Highway in a thirty-one foot motorhome, towing my car with our two-person ocean going kayak tied on the top. Our dog Mariah, with her brave heart, had passed away at the ripe old age of thirteen. Our remaining dog, Gabriel, was my co-pilot. He sat next to me, looking out the front windshield during the long drive south. While on a trip to Anchorage, where I was a speaker at a conference on addictions, I had been offered a job on Vancouver Island in my native British Columbia, Canada. It was time for me to pursue new adventures in the land of my birth.

Jennifer's motorhome on the road south.

Since leaving Alaska I have returned many times to visit family who still live there, to visit David, and to introduce new friends to the wonders of its beauty. My adventures are those of a visitor, not a resident. My new home on Vancouver Island offers many opportunities for outdoor explorations, though usually with less of a life-threatening quality to them. It is nice to enjoy the outdoors in a milder climate. I work in my large garden for ten months out of the year. I live near three large lakes, in which I comfortably swim from May until October (and sometimes a quick dip on New Year's Day!). I enjoy all the months of the year here, and I laugh at the locals who complain about the winter. What winter? We might get a lot of rain in the winter, but I don't care. If we get snow for three weeks out of the year, the locals are delighted, but I am horrified. I go for long walks with my newest German shepherd, whom I have named Miranda, almost every day. I have found my home.

CPSIA information can be obtained
at www.ICGtesting.com
Printed in the USA
FSOW02n0709010316
17544FS

9 781987 985320